"Gail, Gail, ... really did. I ... ...uch to let you go." He tipped ... her chin, staring into brown eyes that appeared so vulnerable and afraid. He kissed her gently. Only when her tears glazed his cheek did he realize the mistake he'd made. *I should have let you go when I could have, for your own good,* he thought. *That would have been a true act of love. But I was selfish and now it's too late.*

A loud knock suddenly sounded on the door. Keith hugged Gail close to him. Again came the thump of a fist, rattling the door on its hinges. He jumped to his feet and raced to the window, searching for an exit from the room. A quick scan of the situation told him the window of the room was far too high. . . . There was no escape.

LAURALEE BLISS, a former nurse, is a prolific writer of inspirational fiction as well as a home educator. She resides with her family near Charlottesville, Virginia, in the foothills of the Blue Ridge Mountains.

Books by Lauralee Bliss

HEARTSONG PRESENTS
HP249—Mountaintop

Behind
the Mask

Lauralee Bliss

Heartsong Presents

To my beloved grandmother and namesake, Laura Schreiber, who so eagerly anticipated this book. I love you, Grandma.

A note from the author:
I love to hear from my readers! You may correspond with me by writing: **Lauralee Bliss**
Author Relations
PO Box 719
Uhrichsville, OH 44683

ISBN 1-57748-613-7

BEHIND THE MASK

Cover illustration by Kay Salem.

one

Gail Shelton despised airline travel. Although she never confessed her fear to anyone, her stomach would twist into painful knots, and a solid lump would form in her throat the moment she boarded an aircraft. Today was no exception. As she walked unsteadily down the passenger tunnel linking the aircraft to the terminal building, she clutched her stomach and swallowed the bile that rose in her throat.

The plane had encountered severe turbulence during its descent through a bank of puffy clouds into Logan International Airport, Boston's thriving air transportation center. Knowing her propensity for air sickness, Gail had pawed through the magazines stuffed inside the pocket of the seat in front of her, searching for the motion sickness bag. She had wanted to keep it close at hand. Next to her had sat an elderly woman, a pair of crochet needles clicking between her fingers, who conversed nonstop about her grandchildren. Beneath the tangle of yarn and needles emerged the beginnings of a blue baby sweater for a new arrival, or so the lady informed her. Gail's mind had buzzed with the woman's incessant chattering until, in desperation, she pulled out an airline magazine and pretended to read the boring articles. The woman had peered over Gail's shoulder at the article on summer gardening, and immediately launched into a diatribe on the varieties of flowers and vegetables she raised. Gail had sensed her irritation rising to the brink of an explosion. She forced down a sharp reply and continued reading.

After the normal flight time had elapsed, the captain

warned his passengers of imminent turbulence as the plane approached Logan. As her seat shook, Gail imagined the plane taking a nose dive into the frothy waves of the Atlantic Ocean, near Boston Harbor. Clutching the armrest in one hand and the motion sickness bag in the other, she wondered if the seats really would serve as flotation devices. Somewhere she had once read that the chance of surviving a crash would be greater if the passenger's seat was located in the tail section of the plane. Aware that her seat was near the nose of the plane, fear formed a hard lump in her stomach. She closed her eyes and began to pray.

At last Gail had felt the plane touch down on the runway. Her stomach had lurched into her throat, then settled into its place. The plane cruised around the maze of runways to finally rest at the gate where she hoped her sister and brother-in-law would be waiting.

Now, as Gail walked briskly down the carpeted passenger causeway, thankful to be done with the dreadful flight, her foot suddenly twisted beneath her. Passengers bumped into her from behind, uttering quick apologies, as Gail looked down to find the heel of her pump resting on the floor. "Great," she muttered, grabbing up the broken heel in disgust. "If anything else goes wrong today, I'm going to tell Dorrie to drive me back to New York and save the visit for some other time."

Hefting her purse and her carry-on, Gail hobbled down to the gate, where cushioned chairs were aligned in rows. Passengers sat reading newspapers or books while waiting for the next flight. Gail scanned the countless faces before her, but recognized none of them. "I'll bet Dorrie forgot I was coming today," she grumbled, limping along on one high heel.

Finally, she heard a voice shout her name, and strong arms grabbed her up in a hefty embrace. "Oh, I'm so glad to see you!" Dorrie cried, whirling Gail around with the force of her affection.

Gail politely wiggled her way out of the embrace. "Look, it's been a long day, Dorrie."

"C'mon, let's go get your luggage then." Dorrie noticed the pointed object in Gail's hand. "What's that?"

"It used to be part of my shoe," she grumbled, showing her older sister the mismatched shoes and the gaping hole where the heel had once been nailed. "This trip hasn't gone right since the moment I left. Some old lady sitting next to me talked the entire time. Then the plane tossed around so much, I almost threw up the bag of peanuts they gave us as a snack."

Dorrie tugged on Gail's left hand. "C'mon, forget your miseries and show me the rock."

"The rock? Oh, you mean my ring."

"Yes, your ring. We aren't going to baggage claim until I see it."

Gail sheepishly brought forth her hand, only to scowl at the chipped nail on her forefinger, a victim of the storage bin that had contained her carry-on. The huge diamond glittered in the lights of the terminal.

Dorrie whistled. "Whooo-eee, now that's some rock! It's at least two carats—maybe ten, by the size of the thing. Is this guy of yours loaded or what?"

"Keith is a very hard worker," Gail quickly answered, withdrawing her hand from her sister's view. "He makes good money repairing computers, now that he's no longer a waiter."

"I'll say he does. Wow! Well, c'mon, Mick's supposed to meet us at the baggage claim after he parks the car."

"Did you bring Jamie?"

Dorrie shot her a grin. "Well, since he is a bit young at ten months to care for himself, I decided to bring him along for the ride."

Gail frowned as she followed her sister through the hordes of people headed for the baggage area. "There you go making fun of me already, and I've only been here ten minutes."

Dorrie hooked her arm through Gail's and gave a squeeze. "I'm not trying to poke fun at you; I was only making a joke. Don't be so serious."

Gail exhaled an exasperated sigh. "If you'd had the kind of day I've had, you'd be serious, too."

"Well, you're here safe and sound, and your nephew can't wait to see his favorite aunt. Plus, I'm dying to hear all the wedding plans. I'm still the matron of honor, right?"

Gail held her carry-on bag up before Dorrie. "I have all the information tucked right in here. Ask me when we get out of this stuffy airport and to a place where I can freshen up. I must look like a wreck." She sniffed her clothing, scrunching up her nose at the odor of plane exhaust. "I've got to change my clothes and put on some perfume after the stench of that airplane."

Dorrie laughed. "Same ol' Gail," she said before adding quickly, "but I wouldn't want you any other way. You did my makeup on my wedding day and taught me everything I needed to know about etiquette. I suppose Mother appreciated the fact that Mick and I finally agreed to have the marriage ceremony inside a church."

"If we had settled on your version of a wedding, the ceremony would've taken place in some backwoods camping area with mosquitoes and flies all over the wedding cake. A church is where people are supposed to get married."

"And we had a great time. I'll never forget it as long as I live."

Gail cast her sister a sideways glance. "I'll bet you won't forget when I tried to catch your bouquet and collided instead with the punch bowl."

Dorrie shrugged as a broad smile crossed her lean features. "Hey, what's a wedding without a few bumbles? You were the star of the show, Gail."

"And so was my yellow bridesmaid's gown with red polka dots, as I remember."

Dorrie laughed merrily.

"But if I hadn't crashed into the punch bowl, I wouldn't have met Keith."

Dorrie paused at that moment to clutch her throat, extend her hand, and act out in distress, "Oh, this is simply dreadful! Look at my lemon yellow gown! I look worse than a child with chicken pox! Please, dearest waiter, would you help me? Oh, you are the most wonderful man!"

Gail couldn't help but smile. "He *was* wonderful—my hero of the night. He helped me to my feet and found a mop to clean up the spill. I'm so glad he doesn't do that job for a living anymore. This computer business is certainly much better."

"I'll say, judging from the size of the rock you're wearing. Well, here we are—baggage claim."

The shrill of a baby in distress halted their conversation. Without a word, Dorrie took off through the crowd, leaving a bewildered Gail to search the sea of faces for her sister. Finally, she noticed the tall form of Dorrie's husband, Mick, standing next to a stroller; he was trying in vain to comfort the screeching ten-month-old. "He sure has a set of lungs on him," Mick was saying as he surrendered the fussy infant into Dorrie's care. "Must come from your side of the family."

"Hey, I don't even know where I'm going and you leave me in the middle of a crowd!" Gail interrupted as she stumbled up, tucking loose strands of curly hair behind her ear.

"Sorry, but this noisy baby needed his mother," Dorrie said, cradling the infant who began sucking on his fist. "Just follow the shrieks and you'll always find Jamie Walters."

"Good to see you again, Gail," Mick said congenially, holding out his hand.

"You can at least give me a hug." Gail approached him with her arms outstretched. "We're related now. And if it weren't for me, you two would have never met."

"Well, you're right about that," he admitted as they embraced.

"Mick, why don't you help Gail find her luggage on the carousel over there while I entertain junior," Dorrie suggested.

"You can't miss my bags," Gail added. "They have big red roses on them. I hope they arrived safely, though. I don't trust these airline carriers one bit. That's why I pack an extra outfit and all my cosmetics in my carry-on, just to be on the safe side."

Gail followed Mick as he skillfully negotiated a path through the crowd. They reached the conveyor belt that was carrying passengers' luggage around a large loop. While waiting for her bags to arrive, Gail studied the profile of Mick Walters. She decided he hadn't changed much since the time they all met in New Hampshire almost three years earlier, while Dorrie and Gail were vacationing in the White Mountains. He still possessed a brawny, muscular frame and honey-blond hair that swept across his forehead. And those fantastic blue eyes. Gail had tried in vain to make Mick her own during that time, but it was plain to see that Mick had fallen head over heels in love with Dorrie. Dorrie and Mick were a perfect match, sharing a mutual interest in the great outdoors that Gail despised with a passion.

Watching Mick as he scanned the conveyor belt for her flower-adorned bags, she decided that while Mick possessed some interesting traits, she felt fortunate to be engaged to the man of her dreams. Both men were similar in stature, but Keith possessed straight dark-brown hair and chocolate-colored eyes that would stare tenderly into her own. At times, he also wore wire-rimmed glasses that gave him a serious appearance. Gail had fallen in love with him the moment he had gallantly arrived on the scene in his crisp white shirt, black vest, and bow tie of a waiter—ready to help her up from the floor after the mishap with the punch bowl during Dorrie and Mick's wedding. At the conclusion of the reception, held near her aunt's home in the Catskill Mountains of New York State, Gail found herself in Keith's company while he cleaned tables. They had made small talk about the evening, after which they agreed to swap phone numbers. To her delight, she discovered that Keith lived with his parents only a short distance from her aunt's home. Several months later, they were reacquainted when Gail returned to visit her aunt. During her stay, Keith invited her out to dinner. On a verandah decorated with ferns and white lights, they sampled a light fare of grilled tuna on a bed of rice pilaf, while sharing with each other their hopes and dreams.

"And you're a part of my dreams now," Keith had told her as the lights in the ferns reflected in his dark eyes. "That's why I've come to a decision. I'm going to look for work down in Westchester County."

"You mean near me? Oh, Keith, that's fantastic!"

"It's about time I got away from here and made a new life for myself." His hand found hers. "And I want you in my life."

After Keith landed a computer repair job, they saw each other almost daily. One thing led to another, until six months later when Keith presented her with the diamond that now decorated her left hand.

"Hey, I said is this yours?" A flowered bag hovered in midair before her eyes, next to Mick's puzzled face.

"Oh, uh. . .yes," Gail answered, checking the name tag.

"A lot on your mind?"

"Just remember how it was when you and Dorrie were engaged."

"Okay, I get the message." Mick hefted up the two bags. "We're looking forward to hearing all about the wedding plans. I know you did a good job organizing ours. If there's anything Dorrie and I can do to make life easier, let us know."

"Thanks." Gail smiled, remembering the day she called to share the news of her engagement with her older sister. Dorrie was ecstatic that Gail had finally abandoned her numerous relationships to settle down with one special guy. The exclamation of approval over the telephone had ricocheted across the room, prompting smiles by both their mother and father, who had welcomed the announcement with hugs and tears of acceptance.

"Oh, how I prayed you would find a special man," Dorrie wrote Gail later in the month. "Our Bible group prays all the time for family members, and you've been on our prayer chain."

Gail read the remark in the letter without the caustic reaction she normally experienced whenever Dorrie espoused her Christianity. Lately, Gail had been thinking about Dorrie and her walk with God. Seeing how Dorrie and Mick led a happy and fulfilled marriage, Gail desperately wanted her own marriage to pulsate with the same joy.

Now she followed the little family out of the terminal building. Mick carried Gail's bags while Dorrie wheeled the stroller with baby Jamie nestled inside. Gail imagined herself walking side by side with Keith, rolling her own baby carriage along with a new little person cuddled beneath a blanket. The wee face and large eyes would peer out to acknowledge the awesome world revolving around him. Tingles of apprehension shot through her at the idea of caring for a little baby. *No doubt Dorrie will make sure I know all about infant care before this visit ends,* she thought.

Once the bags were placed in the trunk and the baby was fastened into his infant car seat, they sped off into the nightmare of tangled traffic that plagued Boston. As Gail watched the buildings of the city shrink in the distance, she recalled a trip that Keith and she had taken to New York City. Amid the tall skyscrapers and the frantic pace of city life, he treated her to dinner and a Broadway play. The lights and music of the play dazzled Gail, but nothing warmed her heart more than when Keith reached for her hand and clasped it in his for most of the production. His touch reached into the depths of her heart, stirring up a wave of love like no one else ever had. Gail certainly had had her share of relationships in the past, but this was different. She knew deep down inside that this was the man she wanted in her life. Not long after the special outing, Keith proposed to her with a similar eagerness for a lifelong relationship.

"I said, how are Mother and Dad?" Dorrie repeated as Gail gazed dreamily out the car window.

"I told you she's a little hard of hearing," Mick said. "I waited five minutes with the baggage before she knew what was going on."

"Oh, love does that to you," Dorrie added. "I remember that after we got engaged, I never heard my boss at the office. He finally got so irritated with me, he broke down and bought a dictation device so he wouldn't have to repeat himself anymore." She turned and yelled to Gail, *"So how are Mother and Dad?"*

Gail cast her an irritated look. "You don't have to scream, Dorrie. I'm sitting right behind you. I can hear everything."

Dorrie shook her head. "Honey, you ain't hearin' nuthin'. You've got the disease, don't you know? It's that long-lost look of love that comes over us women when we've hooked a man. But to be honest, I think he's the one who's got you—hook, line, and sinker."

Gail twirled the diamond ring around her finger, watching the stone reflect delicately colored patterns as the sunbeams streamed through the car window. For once, she agreed with her sister's observation.

"So I'll ask again, how are Mother and Dad?"

"They're doing fine. Mother's worried about the wedding, of course. When I get back from this trip, we'll go shopping for the dress. Dad takes it all in stride."

"He always does," Dorrie agreed. "He's very level-headed."

"Like you."

"Like me?"

"Of course. You're the spitting image of Dad and I'm more like Mother."

Dorrie nodded in agreement. "I can't argue with that. For some reason, Mother could always relate to you."

"And Dad always stuck up for you," Gail hastily answered. When they were younger, Gail often flaunted her relationship with their mother before her older sister. Secretly, she was glad Mother favored her, for Dorrie delved into life with a certain vitality that sparked jealousy within Gail. Now that she sat poised to seal a lifetime commitment with the man she loved, past parental relationships and jealous emotions seemed moot points by comparison.

"Look, I don't think it matters," Dorrie said in a soft voice, echoing Gail's sentiment. "As far as I'm concerned, those years have passed. Now it's on to bigger and better things in both our lives."

Gail could not help but agree, thankful that the years of sibling rivalry and heated debates were only memories. Their lives now traveled similar paths and were filled by the two men who loved them and the challenges yet to be faced.

two

"This is a much better place than where you lived when you first got married," Gail said as Dorrie gave her the whirlwind tour of their new townhouse. "At least it doesn't look like a bachelor pad."

Dorrie cupped a hand to her mouth and whispered, "Between you and me, I couldn't stand those striped curtains Mick used to hang from the bay window in his old apartment. The first day I saw them, I wanted to rip them to shreds and use what was left for dust cloths."

"What's this I hear?" Mick asked as he sauntered in. Blue eyes sparkled with curiosity as he looked first at Gail, then Dorrie.

"Oh, Mick, Dorrie was just telling me how much she misses your old apartment," Gail teased.

Mick folded his arms and pretended to be irritated, despite the tiny smile hovering at the crook of his mouth. "Right. And I'm sure she told you the curtains were not even fit for lining the bottom of a bird cage."

Gail exchanged a look of surprise with her sister before they both erupted into laughter.

"See? I know what you two are talking about," he murmured good-naturedly as he strode out of the guest room.

Gail turned to where she had laid her suitcases in a row on the bed. She unzipped her first suitcase to reveal a mountain of clothing, all neatly folded into small piles with hardly a wrinkle to be found.

"Do you plan on becoming Jamie's nanny and moving in?"

Dorrie asked, pointing a finger at the stack of clothes. "You're only staying for a few days, Gail. You've got enough stuff to last a year!"

"I never know what I'll be doing, so I like to come prepared. Whether I go shopping at the mall or pushing Jamie's stroller outside, I need the right outfit. And of course, the weather here in New England is so unpredictable."

"I hope this Keith character knows the expensive tastes of the dame he's marrying," Dorrie commented, helping Gail hang up her clothes. "I guess it's a good thing he got that new job."

"He loves the clothes I wear," Gail retorted defensively. "He says I'm beautiful. Which reminds me, I must show you the gorgeous bracelet he gave me for Valentine's Day." She reached over to her carry-on bag and inserted a tiny key into the lock. Inside the case she removed a long velvet box. Beneath the lid, buried in matted cotton for protection, lay an exquisite gold bracelet studded with precious diamonds.

Dorrie sucked in her breath like the whirl of a miniature vacuum. "Are those real diamonds?"

"They sure aren't rhinestones! Of course they're real. I just love this bracelet."

"I don't get it. Where does Keith come up with the money to buy this kind of jewelry?"

Gail shrugged as she replaced the treasured piece within the confines of the carry-on. "I told you, he's doing well at his job."

Dorrie's hands flew to her hips. "He can't be doing *that* well. Didn't you tell me he just started this job?"

"He's been there almost a year. Honestly, Dorrie, he's very thrifty. He saves most of his money, unlike me."

Dorrie narrowed her eyes and twisted her lips. "So what else has he given you, if I might be so bold as to inquire?"

"Nothing much. Just an angora sweater, a pair of pearl earrings—"

"Nothing much!" Dorrie interrupted. "Are you kidding me? Earrings, a bracelet, a sweater—all on top of that ring of yours?"

Gail's face contorted into lines of irritation. "What, are you jealous or something?"

"No, I'm not jealous. I just think that—"

"He's very good to me," Gail snapped, slamming down the lid to the carry-on, an action that underscored the vexation rising up within her. "He would give the shirt off his back if someone needed it." She strode across the room and flung herself on the bed, allowing her head to sink into the feather pillow.

"Have you ever met his family? Are they well off?"

Gail screwed her eyes shut. "I don't know if they are. No, I haven't met them yet. Keith says his parents do a lot of traveling with the business they operate. When I return home, I plan on meeting them."

Out of the corner of her eye Gail watched Dorrie settle down on the bed next to her; Dorrie pulled her knees up to her chin in a posture of thoughtfulness. "I hope they don't mind all these wedding plans, considering you've never met them."

"Keith tells me they're excited about the plans. They think I'll make a fine daughter-in-law."

Jamie's scream in the next room brought Dorrie instantly to her feet. "Duty calls. Get yourself some rest. We're ordering a pizza tonight. I'll let you know when it arrives."

Gail mumbled her thanks before rolling on her side and shutting her eyes. She thought of Keith and the night he asked her to marry him. Like a movie displayed in slow motion, she dreamt through every sequence leading up to the big moment when he popped the long-anticipated question.

"But what will your parents think?" Gail gasped, staring at the huge diamond set in gold and nestled inside a red velvet box. "I mean, they've never even met me."

"Don't worry about it," he reassured her as he slipped the ring along Gail's manicured finger. "Everyone thinks it's a great idea. We're meant to be together; you and I both know it. That's all that matters."

Gail relaxed when she heard those words. She examined the diamond setting under the light and thought it was the most beautiful ring she had ever seen. To her, the ring signified much more than a promise of commitment. It signified that a man was willing to love her for the rest of her life.

As she sat absorbed by the ring, Keith traced an index finger down her arm until his hand rested on hers. The sensation sent tingles racing up her back. When she turned, his lips met hers with an urgency that lingered. Gail smiled as she reflected on the sweet encounter. When they parted, he urged her to make a night of it, detailing plans for a glorious encounter in a quaint bed and breakfast to celebrate their engagement. Gail only shook her head and said she wanted to wait until the wedding night.

When Keith asked her why she would cling to such ideas in this day and age, she said, "I guess it has to do with my upbringing. Mother and Dad were very strict about relationships. Dates were fine with them, but there was no stepping over the line." Even then Gail recalled the conversation she had had with her mother as they sat together on a rose-print comforter in her parents' bedroom.

"I know you like boys, Gail," Mother had said, "but there's something I need to share with you. I've never spoken about this until now. Your father and I made a commitment when we were young to wait until our wedding night to show the deepest expression of our love to one another. I know it sounds old fashioned by today's standards, but as my mother told me, intimacy is the one true gift of love you can give to your husband. Don't waste it on some man you will never love. Save yourself for that special night after the wedding when the two of you are together and you see the wedding rings on your hands. It will mean so much more to you that way. Think of it as a special wedding gift for your man that you can't buy for any price."

Gail never forgot those words. Even when Keith applied pressure, suggesting they celebrate their love commitment symbolized by Gail's engagement ring, Gail clung to her belief that she must keep herself pure as a special wedding present.

She snapped open her eyes at the memory of the confused look that crossed his face. He was willing to honor her desire to wait until their wedding night, but Gail sensed he did not understand it.

"Sometimes I wonder myself," Gail murmured, cupping her hands beneath her head. "I know I love Keith, but I just can't take that last step, not after what Mother shared. And Mother and I have always shared things about our lives. I can't just ignore something she believes in so strongly. Besides, she's right. I like the idea of being a wedding present to Keith. He will be so glad I can give him something special on our wedding day, especially after all that he's given me."

At that moment, Dorrie poked her head into the room. The smell of hot pizza wafted in after her. "Supper's on, sleepyhead."

Gail jumped out of bed, ran a comb through her mussed hair, and ventured out to the kitchen where Mick was fastening Jamie into his highchair. Bits of oat cereal lay scattered across the chair's tray.

"He can eat cereal now?" Gail watched in disbelief as Jamie attempted to scoop up the cereal with his tiny fist and stuff it into his mouth.

"He eats like food is going out of style," Dorrie commented, producing a small container of pureed meat and sweet potatoes.

"You make your own food?"

"Of course. I don't trust that junk the stores call 'baby food.' Ugh. Have you ever tasted the stuff?"

Gail shook her head as she slid into a chair Mick held out for her, smiling her thanks in his direction.

"I sampled some at a baby shower the church threw for me," Dorrie continued. "We had to taste different jars of baby food, then write down what we thought they were on a scrap of paper. The one who guessed the most jars of food won a prize."

"Did you win?"

"Not by a long shot. After a few bites of the stuff, I gave up and made a vow that my baby would eat only natural food."

"In fact, Dorrie's excellent at making pureed pizza," Mick added.

Gail wriggled her nose at the image of a pizza slice being transformed into a reddish glob inside a food processor. "Ugh! That's disgusting, Mick."

"I agree," Dorrie echoed as she spooned food into Jamie's mouth, ducking the little fist that continued to push cereal in at the same time. "Go ahead and dig in before it gets cold. I'll be through here in no time. Jamie wins the race when it comes to eating."

Mick bowed his head and offered up a simple prayer for the food, adding a quick prayer for Gail and her wedding plans. When he finished, he slid a slice of pizza onto his plate, then pushed the box across the table to Gail.

"Okay, so let's hear the plans for the big day," Dorrie said.

Gail chewed and swallowed several bites before launching into details of the wedding. She explained the features of the church and the banquet hall she had found close to their parents' home. "And the rent's cheap on Dad. It's hard to afford two huge bashes."

"That's wise. I'm sure it was bad luck that our parents had two girls. We have to buy most everything for the wedding, including the reception, the fancy dress you struggle into only once, the veil. . .the list goes on. Have you bought your dress yet?"

Gail shook her head as she wiped her mouth on a napkin before placing it back across her lap. "Not yet. Mother plans on going dress shopping with me when I get back."

"We could go to a few bridal boutiques here in Boston if you want," Dorrie suggested.

Gail snickered. "You and I don't have the same tastes, Dorrie. Why, you'd probably suggest that I wear a pair of white shorts and a T-shirt to match."

Dorrie spun around, holding the spoon containing orange baby food high in midair. "That's not true. I had all the right attire, including a floor-length gown with a train, and even a veil. I looked very nice for our wedding, didn't I, Mick?"

Mick swallowed a large mouthful of pizza before saying, "You were gorgeous, Dorrie."

"There, you see?"

Gail twirled strands of mozzarella around her finger to form a ring. "I want to buy something special with lots of lace, beads, and a train that stretches halfway down the aisle, just like a princess."

"That costs money. I don't think your cashier's job at the department store will pay for something that extravagant."

"Well, Keith said he'd—"

Dorrie plunked the spoon down on the small table in front of Jamie, who tried to paw it up with his fist and stick it into his mouth. "Don't tell me this dude is going to finance your wedding dress as well." Turning to Mick, she ranted on while Gail stared at her in dismay. "You won't believe the cash this guy doles out. He's bought her jewelry, clothes, and who knows what else. It sounds to me like this guy has robbed a bank or something in the last year, rather than start a new job."

Gail shot out of her seat and threw her napkin on the table. "How can you even say something like that?" she cried. "I'm tired of you questioning the things Keith has given to me out of the goodness of his heart. Excuse me, but I'm going for a walk."

"Gail, wait a minute," Dorrie pleaded as Gail strode out the door and into the twilight. Gail heard the faint echo of her sister's voice calling for her as she marched down the sidewalk, passing a row of townhouses, until she reached a small park established for the residents of the community. Scalding tears dripped down her cheeks. She now regretted coming on this visit. Before she arrived, Gail was excited about the plans for her wedding. Now her joy was dampened by Dorrie's doubts and questions. Gail wiped a hand across her wet cheek and walked over to a swing, where she plopped herself down. *When will Dorrie ever accept the good that comes my way? Either she's jealous of Keith's generous nature, or she only wants to make my life as miserable as possible.* Gail swung to and fro, burdened by her rash of thoughts. She knew Dorrie would never accept her until she uttered vows of Christianity. "Well, if that's what being a Christian is all about," she muttered, "then I don't want any part of it." She closed her eyes, wishing Keith was there to comfort her. She missed his gentle words and strong arms cradling her in times of distress. How could she make Dorrie and others understand that it was simply Keith's love and affection that prompted his outpouring of generosity, and nothing else?

Dorrie appeared from the evening shadows to occupy a neighboring swing. Together, they watched the sun set in the distance before she said, "I remember when I fell off a swing back in school. Fell right on my back. I couldn't breathe. It was the scariest sensation in my life. The teacher had me rushed to the emergency room where they said I had the wind knocked out of me." She glanced over at Gail, who gazed at the ground beneath the swing. "Guess I should've had the wind knocked out of me before I started saying all those things at the dinner table tonight. I'm sorry about what happened. I only want you to know that I care."

"That's not true," Gail muttered. "You want to control my life. You always have."

"I want what's best for you. Look, I've never met Keith. I just want to make sure he's taking care of you right. Maybe once I get to know him, I won't have all these reservations. You know I can't help but be an overprotective sister. I've been that way all my life."

Gail's shoes scuffed up the dirt below the swing. "I know, but I get tired of the lectures and the do's and don'ts. I'm old enough to make my own decisions. I don't need a big sister telling me what to do every waking minute." She lifted her head to see orange and red clouds materialize in the sky, a product of the final rays of the setting sun.

"Okay, you're right. I do get kind of pushy and all. Since this is your big day, you do whatever you want. I'll go along with it without any squabbling. Promise."

Gail cast her a look out of the corner of her eye. "And no more comments about Keith's money?"

"Cross my heart. I'll keep my mouth shut, even though I may need Super Glue to help me."

Gail cracked a small smile and relaxed as her feet scuffed up puffs of dirt. After a moment of reflection, she launched into details of the wedding day, planned for October. Dorrie listened and offered a comment or two but allowed Gail time to air her thoughts.

"It's amazing how much there is to do for one day," Dorrie admitted. "If it will make life any easier for you, I'll help with the invitations. Send me your guest list and I'll even try to have the addresses done in calligraphy by the woman who teaches art in Mick's school."

"That would be nice," Gail agreed, remembering Mick's job as a science teacher in a middle school. "Okay. I ordered them a few weeks ago, so they should be there when I get back to Mother and Dad's."

"Remember, they have to be in the mail about two months before—"

"I know, I know," Gail said impatiently before a yawn erupted on her face.

"I'll bet you're exhausted." Dorrie cupped her hand around Gail's elbow and gently ushered her to her feet. "Let's head back. You can take a nice relaxing shower before you hit the hay."

"Does Jamie still wake up in the middle of the night?" Gail asked as they strolled down the sidewalk toward the townhouse.

"Sometimes. He's pretty good about sleeping through the night, though—it's not like the early days when he'd bawl for food every three hours. I could hardly drag myself out of bed to feed him. Mick would have to get him and I would nurse him half asleep. Sometimes the baby and I would fall asleep together. I'd wake up in the middle of the night with this warm bundle in my arms and wonder where he came from."

Gail laughed until she lapsed into silence, pondering the notion of motherhood. The idea of caring for a little baby unnerved her. She never particularly liked children to begin with. Dorrie often watched the neighbors' children to earn a little extra money, but Gail refused to do it. Kids scared her in many ways. They were overdemanding, unpredictable, and noisy. With the possibility that she and Keith might have children of their own, she felt a strange anxiety course through her. Her body trembled in response.

"What's the matter?" Dorrie asked.

"K–kids."

"Have you and Keith talked about it?"

Gail shook her head. "That's the least of our worries. There's so much to do right now with the wedding and all. As it is, just the idea of caring for some baby gets me all knotted up inside. I mean, if you make a mistake, that's the end."

"Of course it isn't. Look, every first-time mother claims ignorance in some area of baby care. When I found out I was pregnant, I immediately ran out to the store to look at all the baby things for sale. As I stared at the stuff, most of which I had no idea what it was even used for, I prayed, 'Lord, how am I ever going to manage?' "

"But you like kids. You're a natural around them."

"Right. I changed a diaper a few times, maybe gave one or two bottles, and read stories. Having your own is a whole different ball game. Sometimes when you let them howl themselves to sleep, you wonder if you're doing the right thing or if you're damaging them for life. You wonder if you will know when it's time to buy them the next pair of shoes, or move into another diaper size, or what consistency of food they can eat without choking. That's when you really have to trust God."

Gail raised her hands. "Please, no more. I'll just concentrate on my wedding and worry about mothering some other time."

"I think that's a good idea," Dorrie agreed, giving Gail an affectionate squeeze that sent warmth radiating through her. "One thing at a time."

At this moment, Gail could plainly see her sister's caring attitude. In the past, such displays would have been overshadowed by thoughts of Dorrie's sisterly domination over her, or jealousy about Dorrie's accomplishments. Gail realized now that Dorrie's concern for her well-being reflected the Christian commitment she had made long ago.

As Gail readied herself for bed that night, she wondered about Dorrie's Christianity. Many times Dorrie had tried to reach her with the gospel, but Gail batted the idea away as if it were a pesky fly buzzing in her face. She felt religion to be a private matter—something that should be practiced inside a church on Sunday mornings. The idea of living for God every breathing moment seemed hard to swallow. Now she found her feelings changing. Perhaps the idea of a lifetime commitment with Keith opened her heart up to other commitments as well, like the one Dorrie had with God.

Gail had shuffled into the bathroom to remove her makeup when she heard the voices of Dorrie and Mick conversing in the bedroom next door. She dampened a cotton pad with makeup remover and rubbed it across her eyelids to clean off the shadow; she could just make out the word "gang" uttered in the adjacent room. Gail's hand froze. *They must be talking about Mick's work with those gangs in Boston!* She recalled the letters Dorrie had sent to her in the past, explaining Mick's desire to follow in his father's footsteps and reach out to the gangs of inner Boston. Gail shuddered at the thought of confronting such vicious young men, especially after

Mick's father suffered a debilitating gunshot wound at the hand of a gang leader. Yet the conversation sparked her curiosity. She pressed an ear to the wall.

"But I thought Corky was no longer involved in the Vultures gang," Dorrie said in a strained voice.

"Corky says he's not. He only wants others in the Vultures to come and hear about God. That's why he's talking to them about joining my Bible study at the soup kitchen."

"Mick, I don't believe that for a minute. Corky hasn't changed. He's still involved with them. Here you spent all your time reaching out to him; you even went to that drug rehab program with him. I spent nights alone nursing a sick baby while you were tending to his needs. Now he's going right back into the mud again. What's the sense in all this?"

"Dorrie, if Corky was back with the gang, why would he call and tell me he wants to reach them with the gospel? He knows I wouldn't approve of him talking to them for any other reason. Corky thinks of me as his big brother."

Dorrie's voice rose as she said, "Maybe he was just tickling your ear or something."

"No, he isn't. I believe he's sincere."

"Oh, Mick, I want to believe in what you're doing out there in the street. I know it's important to reach the gangs with the love of Jesus. You promised your father you'd carry on his ministry. But I'm really afraid right now. Think of what could happen if Corky or one of the other gang members turns on you when you least expect it."

Gail heard Mick sigh. "Dorrie, you're being irrational."

"I'm not irrational! Maybe I'm the one dealing in reality! I happen to care about us. . .about our family. When it was just the two of us, it was different. I could handle the danger of you working the streets, trying to reach those drugged-out guys. But now you have your son to consider, Mick. You have a family. What will happen to us if that new leader of the Vultures, Odysseus, comes after you like the former leader did with your father? It could happen, you know. And I won't be a widow!"

Silence prevailed until Mick's gentle voice broke through the dark cloud hovering over the tiny home. "So you want me to quit? If you want me to, I will. I don't want you getting this upset. If I'm going to continue in this ministry, we have to agree on it together."

Dorrie exhaled a troubled sigh. "No, I don't want you to quit. I'm just worried that something might happen to you. I only want a vacation from my fear. Is that too much to ask?"

Gail could picture Mick's arms curling around the distraught Dorrie, comforting her fears before kissing away the salty tears sliding down her cheeks. Heaving a sigh, Gail quickly scrubbed her teeth, then made off to the bedroom. She buried herself under a blanket as if to hide from the danger concealed within the conversation. "Thank goodness I will never have to deal with things like that in my marriage," she whispered in relief.

three

"Ah, young Quintin, come right in," the butler said, stepping aside to allow him access into the stately home. "Your father is expecting you in the library."

Quintin frowned as he trudged inside. His sneakers scuffed along the Oriental rugs covering the fine wood floors. He never acknowledged the posh interiors that spoke of great wealth—the crystal chandeliers dangling from every room, the wainscoting of the walls, or the oval glass window at the rear of the home that allowed streams of golden sunshine to bathe the hallway. He walked into the library and took a seat on the leather couch. An odor of cigar smoke and brandy met his nostrils. Across from him sat a man in his mid-sixties, a cigar tucked into the corner of his mouth. Dressed in a dinner jacket, the man was sporting a droopy mustache that rested on the butt of the cigar. As he puffed, his feet resting on a cushioned stool, curls of smoke spiraled toward the ceiling. A glass of brandy sat in a strategic position on the table, close to his fingertips.

The man pulled the cigar out of his mouth and flicked the ash into a tray. "Why didn't you inform me of your engagement?"

Quintin folded his arms across his chest and studied the rows of old books lining the shelf behind the stout figure of his father. The hard voice generated no paternal warmth or concern; this was strictly business.

"I asked you why you didn't tell me."

"Because it's my business, Pop."

The man jammed the cigar back into his mouth. "In case

you've forgotten, your business is my business, and an engagement is a highly important matter that should have been discussed with me first."

Quintin kept his gaze fixed on the books of the library, wondering to himself if anyone had ever bothered to pick the books off the shelf, let alone open the dusty covers to read the contents. He could not remember reading any of the classics growing up, nor could he recall his parents reading to him as a child. An overwhelming sense of loss ensued when he pondered the little things he had missed out on while growing up in a wealthy environment.

"Quintin, are you listening to me?"

Ten, eleven, twelve, thirteen, he counted in a row before proceeding to the next shelf. *Fourteen, fifteen, sixteen.*

"Who is this woman you plan to marry?"

Twenty-one, twenty-two, twenty-three— The counting and the older man's interrogation both came to an abrupt end when the butler entered the library carrying a glass of brandy on a silver tray. Quintin was grateful for the interruption. He took the glass and set it on the table.

His father took a sip of his own brandy before placing it beside him. "There are ways of finding out. If you won't tell me, then you force me to put Grant on the case."

Quintin's brown eyes darted to his father's icy stare that augmented the threat. "Don't you use that buzzard to spy on me," he hissed.

"If you won't tell me what I wish to know, you leave me no choice. I will find out everything. Grant is very good at what he does."

"You call him good? Why, he'd hurt his own mother if the price was right."

"He keeps our operations running smoothly."

"He's a no good—"

"Well, it hasn't hurt you any, has it?" his father spat, straightening in his chair. His teeth smashed the butt of the cigar before he removed the stub with his fingertips. "I see that you've dipped into the accounts, presumably to buy extravagant gifts for your fiancée. And where do you think that kind of money comes from? Men like Grant keep the money flowing. He's good in the business. I'd show him more respect if I were you."

Quintin ground his teeth and looked away. His father began tapping the armrest with a rhythm that disturbed Quintin. The beat reminded him of a countdown to some unknown outcome.

"I assume you will stay and have dinner with me tonight," his father continued. "I had your room prepared. We can discuss this later."

"Actually, I don't plan on staying, Pop. I have a million things to do."

"Such as?"

He grinned before jumping to his feet and jamming his hands into the pockets of his jeans. "Pop, I'm gonna be married. There are plans to be made, things to arrange."

"I don't like your attitude, Quintin. I have not given my permission for this so-called union of yours."

"I'm not asking for your permission, Pop. I'm already engaged, you see."

The older man's lips twisted into a snarl beneath the mustache. "Don't be impertinent with me. You know where things stand. I must know all the facts—who this woman is, who she associates with, what she knows. It could prove dangerous."

"Pop, she doesn't know a thing about us. There's no need to worry."

"And how do you plan on keeping everything from her?

There will come a time when she will be exposed to—"

"I don't want her knowing anything. You keep your silence pretty well in your elite circle of friends. They know nothing about what we do. In fact," he added with a hint of sarcasm, "you pride yourself in all the secrecy."

"And I hope my son possesses the same discretion," the older man answered in a guarded voice. "Now, I insist that I meet this young lady as soon as possible. We will set up an appointment."

Set up an appointment. Quintin nearly laughed out loud. *Sounds like a doctor trying to cure a disease that might infect the business.* "Sorry, but I just don't have the time. Now, if you'll excuse me, I have to get going." He turned to leave the library.

"Quintin!"

He ignored the plea. In the dark hall outside the library doors, Quintin bumped into a short man with black, greasy hair and a face pitted from a severe case of acne as an adolescent. A grin on the scarred face revealed a gaping hole in a row of teeth that filled the thin-lipped mouth.

"Watch where you're going," Quintin muttered.

"If I were you, I'd watch where *you* are going, you young fool," the man retorted.

"Grant, you were born to live in a hole, not among decent people."

"I see only that the big boss's son is headed for trouble. You of all people should know it's unwise to go against your father's wishes."

Quintin narrowed his eyes. "And who are you to tell me what to do? You have a lot of nerve, standing outside the door listening to our conversation. Nothing's private anymore with you slithering around like some snake."

"I'm not your father's right-hand man for nothing."

"That's for sure. Anyone making the kind of money you do is bound to stick close to the source. But I won't have you breathing down *my* neck."

Grant's hand brushed open his sports jacket, exposing the hilt of a pistol he wore in a leather holster. "I'll say it once more. You would be wise to listen to your pop and do what he says, like an obedient son. Look at it this way. Before a guy enters into a marriage, isn't it normal to have the bride-to-be meet the father of the groom? Won't you bring all kinds of suspicion down on yourself if you refuse? What will your bride say?"

"You're made of slime, you know that? Pure slime."

"I see only that your father's wishes are carried out."

"You see only to your own self-interest in this game. If you will excuse me, I'll do as I see fit. Now get out of my way."

"Stubborn fool," Grant muttered, glaring at Quintin with beady black eyes.

Quintin refused to acknowledge the threatening look of his adversary. With his gaze fixed on the exit, he marched down the hall and out the door, breathing a sigh of relief at having escaped the darkness within the mansion. The bright summer flowers, arranged in beds around the circular driveway, did little to ease the anxiety in his heart. If it were not for the strength of love binding him to his fiancée, he would never allow her to enter into this corrupt family of his. Yet he could not fathom life without her. Now, with Grant involved, he might have to risk letting her visit his father—to prevent Grant from following her every move.

Quintin climbed into his car and swiftly drove out the tree-lined drive leading to the estate. He checked his rearview mirror often to make certain he wasn't being followed. Many times in his travels he sensed the wily Grant in the dark corners, the man's black eyes glinting, his ears attentive to every whisper. He knew Grant had somehow discovered the news of his engagement and had immediately informed his father. Quintin was thankful, though, that his fiancée had not found herself confronted by the man.

With his father threatening to use Grant as a spy if he did not agree to a meeting, Quintin knew he had no choice. There was never a choice for him when it came to his father's ultimatums. Pop was the boss. Everyone listened to the boss and followed his directions—or suffered the consequences. *Including me,* he thought miserably. *Can I put her through all this, though? Am I being selfish by marrying her, knowing it might place her in harm's way? But I love her so much! I have to marry her. I must never let her know who we are or what we do. If I want her safe and in my arms until death do us part, then I must lock the secret of the family within me and keep it from her forever.*

Quintin drove to the next town, where he promptly located a phone booth at a convenience store. He withdrew from his pocket a slip of paper upon which he had written a phone number, and punched in the digits, eagerly anticipating the sound of her voice. Instead, the mechanical whirl of an answering machine met his ear, along with a strange message that ended with the words, "And remember, God cares about you."

Quintin frowned. He hung up without leaving a message. He recalled in numerous conversations with his fiancée that her sister was a deeply religious person. He wondered how she could visit under that kind of pressure. To him, there was nothing worse than people spouting off their religion in an attempt to convert others. He would never admit that the reverent messages had convicted him at times. One day, he found the Ten Commandments, printed in some small pamphlet, tucked underneath the windshield wiper of his car. He was ready to wad the paper up into a tight ball when he started reading the words. "Thou shalt not kill; Thou shalt not steal; Thou shalt not covet another's belongings; Thou shalt not commit adultery." He sucked in his breath. *How many of those commandments have I broken, let alone my family? Is God angry about all the deceit and disobedience?* Quintin had brushed the thoughts aside as he pitched the convicting paper to the ground, unsure if God even existed.

Now the message on the answering machine prompted him to think again about the existence of God. If there was a supreme being, why did He allow man to commit evil? And if he was supposed to obey all those rules in the Bible, why didn't this God send down a lightning bolt from heaven and strike him dead for disobeying them? Perhaps Quintin had grown to believe himself invincible, like his father had. Quintin knew his pop refused to believe that the authorities, or even God Himself, could catch him in his misdeeds and deal the punishment he rightly deserved. He could have won the award for best actor with his efforts to mask his sins with occasional acts of kindness; actions designed, Quintin knew, to conceal from others what lay buried beneath the surface. Quintin closed his eyes and sighed. He was much like his father in many respects. That fact gnawed at him fiercely.

ะ

"I really enjoyed myself," Dorrie announced to Gail as they arrived back at the townhouse, burdened with shopping bags from a trip to the mall. "I'm so glad you convinced me to buy some new outfits."

"Let's face it, Dorrie. After a while, jeans and T-shirts just don't cut it." Gail hurried into the back bedroom and tossed her bundles on the bed. She could hear Dorrie checking the answering machine in the living room, and promptly ran back for a report. "Any messages for me?"

Dorrie shook her head. "Mick called. He's going to be late

tonight at the soup kitchen. Then someone else called but didn't leave a message."

Gail frowned. "Oh. I was hoping Keith would call me. I miss him so much."

"I imagine you do." Dorrie set to work opening up an activity board she had purchased for Jamie at a toy store. She placed it down on the carpet and watched the infant boy reach out his tiny hands to investigate the knobs and buttons. "You wouldn't believe the phone bill Mick and I piled up while I lived on Long Island and he lived here in Boston. I had to work overtime just to pay the bill."

"It's nice that Keith lives close by. I don't have to worry about phone calls, unless it's to plan an outing or something. I get to have the real flesh-and-blood guy all to myself."

"Yeah, that must be nice." Dorrie lapsed into quiet thoughtfulness as she picked up the bags and carried them to the master bedroom. Gail followed to help her hang up a new dress and fold some shirts.

"So is Mick going out on the streets tonight?"

Dorrie whirled at the sound of her voice. "You scared me! I didn't know you were there. Yes, Saturday nights are his busiest time. He works in the soup kitchen with a guy named Harry. They serve food that arrives from the area restaurants. Sometimes it's pans of macaroni and cheese, or lasagna, or luncheon meat. I used to help out once in a while, before I had Jamie. When Mick gets done there, he walks the streets and hands out tracts."

Gail picked up a new blouse from the bed and used a pair of shears to snip off the tags. "I. . .I wasn't trying to be nosy or anything, Dorrie, but I couldn't help overhearing you guys talking the other night. You don't want him working with those gangs anymore, do you?"

Dorrie's arms stiffened into robotic movements as she

forced a hanger through the neck of a dress. "Sometimes it's not a question of what I want, but what God wants."

"Well, you'll probably faint when you hear this, but I happen to agree with what you said. But I don't think God would want Mick sacrificing you and Jamie for a bunch of weird kids that smoke pot and kill each other."

Dorrie sighed. "It's hard to know what to think. Sometimes I try to rationalize it, but I only end up more confused. I'm trying to trust God for our safety."

"I'm glad I don't have to worry about things like that," Gail remarked. "I couldn't handle it if Keith found himself in danger every night. I mean, if something happened to him, I'd die, too."

Dorrie grew silent as if pondering the statement. Gail sensed that her sister experienced similar thoughts often when Mick was absent. Perhaps she had considered what life would be like for her and little Jamie if a gang member were to shoot Mick—like the bullet fired into his father's brain six years ago. The injury had bound the older man to a life in a wheelchair at an extended-care facility.

Tears welled up in Dorrie's eyes. She turned away to avoid displaying her emotion. "I have thought a lot about it," came the muffled voice as she finished hanging her new clothes inside the closet. "I've spent many sleepless nights worrying about him. I look behind my back often to make sure that none of those gang members are stalking Jamie and me. I know I shouldn't live my life dreading what's around the corner. I guess that's why I want Mick to quit the work so I can just relax for once in my life."

"I think your reactions are very normal," Gail offered. "You love your husband and your son. There's nothing wrong with that."

Dorrie turned at that moment and threw her arms around

Gail. "Oh, Gail, I had a feeling we'd grow closer once you were married, but now I can see it's already started. Long ago when we took that camping trip of ours to the White Mountains, I wanted to have a special relationship with you. I guess we both had some maturing left to do before that could happen. Now we're entering stages in our lives where we can help each other."

"I think so too, Dorrie," Gail agreed, surprised by the tears swimming in her own eyes. "But I know I need to grow up some more. I mean, I still get jealous of you sometimes. I used to think you were out to get me with all that religious talk of yours. But I know, deep down inside, that you really care about me."

Dorrie nodded. "It's like what Mick and I decided to put on our answering machine for people who need to hear the message. We say on the machine that God cares about you. I could not begin to care for you like I should without God's help."

"Yeah," Gail said slowly, knowing deep down her sister's words were true.

"And God does care. Sometimes I need to grasp the whole meaning of that, especially where Mick's mission field is concerned. I need to have a heart for those gang members, like God does. Then I wouldn't feel so frightened. You know, most of those poor kids come from broken homes or abusive situations. They have never known the love of a family. They use drugs and alcohol as their escape, and then end up committing violent crimes because they have nothing else to do with their lives. It's amazing to think that God really cares about them. He sent Jesus to die for them as He did for all of us, so we can share in God's love. That's the message Mick takes to them—a love that every heart longs to have."

Gail quietly listened. In the old days her pride would have drowned out the religious talk. As she observed Dorrie's vulnerability while searching for comfort within the words, Gail found herself listening instead of reacting. Dorrie was reaching deep into the meaning of her faith, searching for something to grab hold of that might lift her out of her pit of fear. For all of Dorrie's steadfast convictions, it amazed Gail to see how much her sister needed to understand the purposes of God in her life almost as much as Gail did herself.

Later that night, after she had gone to bed, Gail heard the door to the townhouse open and close and the weary footsteps of Mick slowly ascend the stairs. Gail squinted at the lighted numerals on the clock to see the time—midnight. She sighed and was fluffing her pillow when the voices in the next room caught her attention.

"You don't have to worry anymore, Dorrie," Mick said as his shoes hit the wall opposite Gail's room. "I told Harry I'm quitting."

"What?" Dorrie cried, the tone betraying her astonishment.

"God closed the door to this whole ministry. Nobody cares to hear the gospel. I was all set to have the Bible study tonight with these guys Corky promised would come. No one showed."

"Oh, Mick, I'm so sorry."

"They were too busy counting the goods they plan to sell to pay for their drugs. Corky told me all about it, how the Vultures sell all the stuff they steal to some guy who buys them out. Then they have loads of cash for their drugs and booze. He told me about the time the lights went out in Boston—how they had a field day looting the stores, making off with televisions, stereos, the works. He said they made enough cash in one night to buy crack for months. The Vultures have the reputation for being the richest gang in the 'hood,' as Corky put it. And for some reason, God wants me to reach out to them. It's ludicrous."

Gail shivered as she crawled deeper into her blankets.

Mick continued. "I tell you, Dorrie, when I heard that, I thought to myself, what's the use? Those guys think they have everything. They don't need God when they can nurse their troubles away with a good snort or a shot of hard liquor."

"Mick, just because no one came to the Bible study doesn't mean you should—"

"Yes, it does," he interrupted. "I'm quittin' this whole thing. I feel bad because I promised Dad I would reach out to that gang, but I can't go on like this."

Gail heard Dorrie exhale a troubled sigh. "I know I'm partially to blame for this. I'm sorry about what I said. I'm trying to give God my anxiety. I don't want my fear leading you away from the path He has planned for you."

"Dorrie, it isn't just you. It's the rejection you feel when someone wads up the tract you give to them in love, then lights a match to it. It's that kid who would rather inject drugs into his veins after hearing the gospel preached than getting right with God."

"Well, what about Corky? Are you giving up on him too? He could use a Bible study, probably more than anyone right now."

Gail could hear the sneering chuckle rise in Mick's throat. "You never liked Corky anyway, so what does it matter? You always thought he was pretending or something just so he could hang around with the gang."

"Well, I was wrong about that," Dorrie said softly. "Only God knows what's going on in his heart. It's our responsibility to see that he continues to grow in the ways of the Lord. Please, Mick, I'm sorry I haven't supported you."

"Dorrie, I've already told you it's not that. I love you and Jamie. I want us to be a family and do family things together."

"But Mick, you know those kids on the streets. They're

looking for a big brother who'll be like family to them. As God helps me, I'll share you with them because I know you can reach their hearts. Corky is proof of that."

"Corky is only one insignificant acorn off a three-year tree of hard work. It isn't enough for me."

"Then I'll ask you one more question. Did God tell you to quit this ministry to be with Jamie and me?"

Gail lay silent in her bed, waiting for what seemed like an eternity for Mick's answer.

"No. God didn't tell me to quit."

"Then we'd better both obey Him and keep going. We're both learning in all this. I think we've reached a crossroads in your work. When you give all this over to God and wait on Him, I think you're going to reap a great harvest. Just don't keep looking to your own power to make these young people come out of their shells and reach out to God. Allow God to work in their hearts. We need to be ready when the opportunity comes."

Mick's voice softened to a mere whisper as Gail strained to hear. "I love you so much, Dorrie. As always, you know the right thing to say at the right time." She heard a soft ruffle of blankets, followed by silence.

Gail lay back on her pillow, her eyes wide, thinking about what had been shared. She wondered what kind of conversations she and Keith would have in the middle of the night. "Well, I'll tell you one thing," Gail muttered, flipping over on her side, "we're going to be a normal couple. We'll go to work, come home, fix dinner, and cuddle in each other's arms. I couldn't possibly live on the edge like Dorrie and Mick. Thank goodness I'll soon be home, safe and sound with the one I love."

four

The following evening, Gail kissed her sister, brother-in-law, and nephew good-bye before heading through the security check-in for her flight back to New York. As Dorrie clung to her, whispering farewell and voicing her excitement about the upcoming wedding, Gail sensed the bond that had formed between them. Dorrie seemed eager to help in any way she could, and promised to arrive early the week of the wedding to help with any last-minute details.

Gail glanced over her shoulder once more as she boarded the plane, and saw the pair wave a final farewell, the baby stroller nestled between them. She wondered what life had in store for her during the next few months. She located her seat adjacent to a small oval window; through the window she could see the maze of lighted runways. As she sat down, she sensed a renewed eagerness to see Keith. He had finally called her in Boston and expressed a longing to see her. The sound of his rich voice expounding on his love for her had caused goose bumps to break out on her skin. He also mentioned that he had arranged for them to have an intimate dinner at their favorite place, after spending a whole day together. Gail felt fortunate to have netted such a thoughtful man. There was no one like him in the entire world. As she leaned her head against a spongy pillow given to her by one of the flight attendants, a delightful thought crossed her mind: Soon she would have him forever.

❧

A taxi dropped off Gail and her bags at the modest ranch home in Westchester County that she shared with her parents.

Once inside the front door, her mother immediately informed her of the arrangements she had made for the wedding. "Oh, and I found the perfect dress. You must go with me tomorrow to see it."

Gail gulped. "But Mother, Keith and I are spending the whole day together—we've already planned it. We have so much to talk about. Then we're going out to dinner."

"But there's a special sale going on at this boutique, and you really shouldn't miss out on the fabulous price."

Gail had to admit she was curious about what her mother had discovered in her absence. She decided to call Keith and see if he might be able to meet later that day.

"Gail, I was really counting on us being together all day," he protested. "I even took time off work."

Gail sighed as she played with the engagement ring on her finger. "Oh, I wish there was some way to work around this. Mother says I really must see this dress while it's still on sale. If I like it, I don't dare pass up such a deal. Can't we meet afterward?"

"Well, look—I really need to see you tonight. How about meeting me at Doc's?"

"What, right now?"

"Yes, right now. There's something I have to discuss with you."

"Well, uh. . . ," Gail began, wondering what could be the reason for his insistence. "I just got home, and Mother is—"

"Look, forget about your mother and concentrate on me for a change. Now meet me at Doc's." He then added, "Please."

The receiver clicked in her ear. She winked back the tears that invaded her eyes. Why was Keith so angry? She had never known him to be irritable unless he'd had a run-in with a coworker at the computer company. *That must be it,* Gail decided, trying not to read too much into the conversation.

He's had a bad day at work. It happens to all of us, I guess.

When Gail announced her plan to meet Keith at Doc's, a cafe down on Main Street, her father cast her a concerned look. "At this time of night? You just got home."

"Yes," her mother interjected. "And we also need to discuss ideas for the flowers and the cake so we can stop by those shops after we go to the wedding boutique."

"Look, I'll be back as soon as I can. It sounded kind of urgent. I need to borrow the car, Dad, if that's all right."

"Just be careful. I don't like the idea of you roaming the streets this late at night. Go straight there and come straight home."

"I will." Gail hurried off to the car, not wishing to be late. She hoped the time with Keith would be more pleasant than the phone conversation they'd just had. Her hands trembled as she steered the car out onto the highway; she was wondering why he had requested their impromptu meeting. "I only hope he's not having second thoughts about our engagement," Gail said to herself. She swallowed hard, forcing down the anxiety that crept up within her. With a shake of her head, she tossed back a mound of curly hair. "Now who's afraid? Keith said he loved me. He told me so on the phone while I was in Boston. There's nothing to worry about."

She arrived at Doc's and through the window saw Keith sitting at a table in the far corner of the establishment, fidgeting with a cup of coffee while glancing out the window. His glasses lay on the table. She watched him draw his fingers across his eyes, then lift the cup of coffee and take a swallow. Gail inhaled a deep breath, checked her appearance in a lighted compact inside her purse, then walked into the shop with her head high and a smile on her face.

Keith's head popped up when the front door creaked, announcing her arrival. He jammed on his wire-rimmed glasses and pulled out a chair for her.

"I. . .I came as soon as I could," Gail managed to say while scanning the strange expression on his face.

His eyes darted to the window. "You didn't see anyone hanging around outside, did you?"

"No." Her muscles tightened at the mere suggestion. "Is something the matter?"

"No, nothing's the matter. I just know there's plenty of weird people out this time of night." He lifted his mug. "You want some coffee?"

Gail shook her head. "I'll never get to sleep if I drink coffee this late in the evening."

"Well, I don't want that to happen. You need your beauty sleep." He cracked a faint smile as he saluted her with his cup, then took a hefty swallow. "I could drink this stuff all night and it would have no effect on me. Even when I drank a gallon of it while pulling an all-nighter studying for an exam, I still fell asleep with my head in my textbook." He leaned back in his chair and folded his arms. "How was your flight from Boston?"

"It was nice. I like flying in the evening. There's no crowds and the Manhattan skyline is beautiful."

"How is your sister and her family?"

"We had a nice time together. Jamie is so cute. I think this was the first time Dorrie and I were actually civil with each other. It seems like all we've done our entire lives is fight over some silly thing. Now she sees that I'm mature, ready to handle marriage and all." Gail felt a sudden shyness at the words. She dropped her head to acknowledge the ring glittering on her left hand, hoping she was mature enough to handle whatever the future held.

Keith focused his gaze on his coffee mug. "Well, that's primarily what I wanted to talk to you about."

Fear rose up within her in response to these words. *Oh no, he is having second thoughts. That's why he was so cross with me on the phone.*

"I think it's time you came home to meet the family."

Gail exhaled a sigh of relief before breaking out into giggles. "Is that all? Oh, Keith, you had me scared to death!"

His head jerked, sending his wire-rimmed glasses scooting back up his nose. "About what?"

"Well, you get crazy ideas running through your head when the one you love asks for a meeting this late at night. Couldn't you have told me this tomorrow?"

"Well, I wanted to see you. I missed you, you know." His hand reached out and clasped hers tightly.

"I missed you, too. I guess that's reason enough, huh?" She smiled, watching his dark brown eyes soften into a mist that spoke of his feelings for her. "When am I supposed to meet them?"

"I was thinking we could drive up next weekend."

"Okay. That should be fine, as long as I can get someone to switch weekends with me at the store. I can stay with my aunt. She gets lonely in that big house of hers. She'll love the company."

Keith glanced away for a moment. "I hope you like. . .well, my family."

Gail chuckled. "I'm sure I'll love your family, Keith! I love you! I only hope they'll like *me.*"

"Just be your ol' bubbly self and everything will go fine. Don't try to be someone you're not." He grew serious then, and picked up his mug to throw the rest of the coffee down his throat.

They conversed for a while longer, about wedding plans and other things, until Gail noticed the late hour on her watch. "I'd better get home before Dad has a coronary." Keith walked her to the car parked across the street. Before she could drop into the driver's seat, his arms curled around her.

"I really missed you," he said softly. "I'm glad you're back."

"I'm glad to be back, too."

His lips were soft and warm against hers when they kissed. When they parted, a smile lit her face. They embraced once more before she sank down into the driver's seat.

"I'll call you," he promised, waving farewell as she pulled away from the curb and headed down the lighted street.

❧

Keith frowned when he thought of the words he had spoken to Gail that night. *Don't try to be someone you're not.* "Yeah, and what about me?" he mumbled, scuffing his shoe across the pavement. "Gail doesn't even know who I am." He turned and was headed down the sidewalk toward his car when suddenly a deep voice called to him from the shadows of a dark storefront.

"Wise decision."

Keith wheeled to find Grant walking out of the murky shadows toward him, a cigarette in his fingers. His grin displayed the gaping hole created by several missing teeth.

"What are you doing here?" Keith growled. "Quit following me."

Grant only shook his head and mouthed a tsk-tsk as he flicked the ash of his cigarette onto the ground. "You know I can't do that, Quintin. This is what I'm paid for, to make certain you do what's right. And you made a wise decision, involving the boss in your wedding plans."

"I'm telling you right now to beat it back up north where you belong. If you so much as show your ugly face around Gail, you'll have me to answer to."

Grant only chuckled as he blew a ring of smoke into the air.

"Just don't press your luck, bub. I mean it. Stay away from

Gail. In fact, stay away from us, period." Keith marched off, only to slow as he reached the corner. A great heaviness fell onto him when he considered the consequences of bringing Gail into his corrupt family. "What am I doing?" he wondered aloud. "How can I drag Gail into the middle of all this? How can I enter a marriage relationship with enough baggage to fill the cargo hold of a 747? Do I love her so much that I'm willing to risk my family's involvement in our marriage and our lives?" He paused to consider the question before kicking at a stone that tumbled away into a gutter. There seemed to be no way of escaping his treacherous family. "But there has to be. I won't let Pop take control of our marriage. I can't. There has to be a way out, a quick and easy way for us to be together without his influence in our lives. Then we can get far away from here—from all the corruption, and men like Grant."

≈

Gail was surprised by Keith's gloominess as they traveled together to the Catskill Mountains of New York State, home both to her aunt and to Keith's family. She tried to engage him in conversation, describing her trips to several stores to investigate flower arrangements and sample wedding cakes. "I want you to help me decide on the best flowers and cake after we get back," Gail urged, poking him in the arm to elicit a response. "Tell me what kind of cake you like best. Mother and I sampled a carrot cake that was just out of this world. And the flowers. I can't decide if I want roses in my bouquet or white gardenias. The flowers in the florist's shop smelled just heavenly."

Keith shrugged his shoulders. "Aren't flowers and cake something the bride's supposed to worry about?"

"But I thought you might want some input. I mean, this is *our* wedding, not just mine."

He kept his eyes focused on the road before him as he

stirred in the driver's seat. Finally, he licked his lips and said, "Gail, to be honest, I just don't know about this."

"What?" she asked. "You've been quiet ever since we started this trip. Is something wrong?"

"Well, I'm kind of having second thoughts about throwing a big shindig and all. In fact, I really think we should just skip all these fancy arrangements and elope."

Gail's eyes widened in alarm. "Elope! Are you kidding? Why?"

"It just seems like you're going through an awful lot of hassle for one day. We know we love each other and want to get married. I don't see the reason behind flowers, cakes, churches, and everything else. Then you have to deal with family, which is another headache."

Gail blinked, surprised by his change of heart. She assumed Keith, to whom she had confided her heartfelt dreams, would realize the importance of having a fancy wedding with all the trimmings. Every night, she went to bed thinking of walking down the aisle dressed in a gown sparkling with beads, with a long train that stretched behind her for miles. She pictured the band playing a romantic melody as they danced their first waltz, and her feeding Keith a piece of wedding cake lovingly cut with a silver knife. "I don't understand, Keith. Why this sudden change? I thought we agreed to have a nice wedding. The families are expecting it."

"That's the whole point, the family bit. It's hard to explain. I guess I'm just uptight about you visiting my home. You see, I come from a very strict household. They hold to strange ideas and, well, strange customs, I guess you could say. I don't want to see you or your family hurt by anything my family might try to do."

Gail stared at Keith in confusion as a ruddy flush filled his cheeks. Bony white knuckles protruded from his hands as he gripped the steering wheel. "Keith, really, what can be so bad about your family? They're only people, like you and me. If I'm going to be a part of your family, then I should try to knit myself in with them somehow."

"No!" he shouted. "That's the whole point. I don't want you knitting yourself in. I don't want you involved with them in any way, shape, or form."

She blinked in astonishment at the caustic tone of his voice. "Is there something you aren't telling me?"

"No!" he said again in a voice that sent Gail shrinking in her seat. She shifted her attention to the scenery whirling past the car window. She heard a sigh, followed by fingers reaching for her hand. "Look, I'm sorry I lost my cool. I just want you to know that I've reached a decision about us. I feel it would be better for all parties involved if we pull into the next big town and find a justice of the peace to marry us. Then we can go on with our lives in some remote location, away from any family interference."

Gail watched her dream of a fairy-tale wedding slowly disintegrate before her eyes. "B–but Keith, I already put a deposit on the dress, and the veil I want reaches to the. . . ," she paused when he steered the car into a rest area.

After parking the car in an isolated spot, he leaned back in his seat. Quietly, almost inaudibly, he said, "Gail, I'll be blunt with you. If we don't elope, then we don't get married. It's that simple."

His words numbed her senses. "B–but why can't we have a wedding?" she wailed. "You haven't told me why! You said this has to do with your family, but—"

"Gail, just trust me, please." He removed his glasses and threw them on top of the dashboard. "I love you enough to do it this way. I've thought about it ever since the night we left Doc's. I knew I had to come to a decision, as painful as this is turning out to be." He reached out a finger to gently dry the tear gliding down her cheek. "I love you more than life itself, but there are certain things I cannot have you involved with, chief of which is my family. I wish you could see that I'm only trying to protect you."

Gail fumbled for her purse, unzipped it, and withdrew a crumpled tissue. "I don't know what to think, Keith. We've known each other for a long time and you've never once mentioned this problem with your family. Now that we're ready to finalize the arrangements, and I'm ready to meet them for the first time, you lay all this on me." She blew her nose. "It just doesn't make sense."

"Gail, do you love me?"

"Of course I do. What a silly question."

"If you love me, then please marry me right now and don't ask any more questions."

Gail stared at her engagement ring, wondering if she was ready to make a commitment to a man who had suddenly turned her life upside down in a matter of a few minutes. Yet her heart knew there was only one answer to give to the one who occupied her thoughts almost every moment of the day. Softly she said, "I'll marry you today, if that's what you want."

"Great!" he exclaimed, straightening in his seat as he turned the key in the ignition. "We'll drive to Poughkeepsie and find a justice of the peace right now."

Gail sat still in her seat, numbed by the abrupt turn of events. She was thankful to see Keith's happiness return, but the situation did little to relieve the turmoil in her own heart. There would be no wedding music, no fancy dress, no well-wishers to congratulate her on her special day, no beautiful arrangement of cheeses and fruits for the reception. There would only be the impersonal ceremony conducted by a justice of the peace, a signature on a piece a paper legalizing their marriage, and all her dreams buried in the dust.

She could hardly hear Keith as he tried to brighten the situation by promising a beautiful honeymoon in the Caribbean, complete with moonlit walks on the beach, a boat ride to a deserted island, and anything her heart desired. Gail tried to gulp down the lump in her throat and listen to his plans, but nothing could remove her disappointment. *My heart's desire was a beautiful wedding like Dorrie's,* she thought sadly. *Now it's gone because of his family. What could possibly be so wrong that we must elope? Maybe his family doesn't want him marrying someone like me.* She paused to consider this reasoning. *Maybe they expected him to marry someone they know and like. I guess Keith believes we must elope to avoid some major blowup.* She cast him a glance out of the corner of her eye and saw the smile on his face. At least Keith wanted to demonstrate his love by marrying her against his family's wishes. She made up her mind to remain positive about the situation, praying that her heart would find healing from this painful blow.

five

"Well, it's over." Keith tucked an arm around Gail as they walked down the sidewalk toward the car. "It's official. We're now Mr. and Mrs. Hampton."

"There wasn't much to it," Gail said meekly. The ceremony was just as awful as she knew it would be. The simple affair was presided over by a stern justice who demanded his fee up front before he would conduct the marriage. His secretary stood in as a witness with a blank face of indifference. The office where the ceremony took place smelled of paper and ink. The only plant in the room was a potted fern, decorating an obscure corner. Gail never felt so disappointed in all her life. Since they had not purchased wedding bands beforehand, the secretary hastily fashioned two makeshift rings out of paper clips, which they exchanged at the appropriate time. Keith promised after the ceremony that they would go at once to a jewelry store and buy a pair of rings, but Gail only wanted to leave town as soon as possible.

"Why don't we find ourselves a cozy place to spend our wedding night?" he suggested. "Maybe a nice bed and breakfast. Would you like that?"

Gail shrugged her shoulders as she twirled the paper clip wedding band around her finger. Nothing seemed to matter anymore. The way this day had gone, she would probably have to settle for a night in some cattle barn. Keith could not help but notice her mood and tried his best to alleviate it by promising everything but the stars in exchange for the hasty ceremony.

"I just hope you're happy," she mumbled as they walked past a jewelry store.

"Of course I am. This is the happiest day of my life. I only wish I could make you happy." He glanced back to see the store sign and the ornamental jewelry pieces shining in the windows. "C'mon," he urged, tugging on her hand. "Let's go pick out those wedding bands right now."

"I don't know if I want. . . ," Gail began as they entered the store.

"May I help you?" inquired a matronly woman who stood behind a showcase that displayed a large assortment of silver and gold wedding bands.

"We want to see the most expensive wedding bands you have in stock," Keith informed her, oblivious to the astonished look on Gail's face.

The woman arched an eyebrow. "Do you have the money to request such a thing, young man?"

"Lady, I wouldn't be asking if I didn't." He waved his checkbook in front of her face. "I can sign over any amount I wish. Trust me."

"Keith. . . ," Gail began, but he ignored her.

The woman brought out several different styles of rings to try on, including a set with a price tag of ten thousand dollars. The solid gold bands, decorated with sparkling diamonds, took Gail's breath away.

"We'll take those," Keith said and promptly wrote out the check.

Gail was beside herself as she watched him write out the huge sum before handing the check over to the woman. All at once, the recollection of Dorrie's comments concerning his pricey gifts flashed into her mind. She tried to bury her uneasiness when the woman handed them the expensive purchase in a velvet box.

"There you are," Keith told her. He slipped the ring on her finger, followed by a kiss. "Now do you feel like Mrs. Hampton?"

"I guess so," Gail murmured. The large diamond ring and glittering wedding band on her finger made her entire hand sparkle like expensive cut crystal in the sun. Gail hid her hand beneath the arm Keith offered her and strolled with him down the sidewalk. "Do you mind if I ask you something?"

"Shoot."

"Where did you get that kind of money?"

He paused before he replied, "I saved it."

"You saved ten thousand dollars? Why, it can take years to save up that much money!"

"Don't worry about it. I have it and that's all you need to know." He gave her a squeeze. "Besides, you're worth every penny and more. Look, there's our car. Let's get going and find a place to spend the night."

❧

Gail tried to relax at the quaint bed and breakfast they had discovered during their travels, but the events of the day weighed heavily upon her. Keith appeared ready and eager to give of himself in every way, but Gail spurned his affection and curled up instead in an easy chair. She stared out the small window at the glimmering street lights below, numbed by all that had happened.

"Don't you want to be with me?" Keith asked. When she refused to answer, he said, "Look, if I'm not mistaken, you promised me a gift on our wedding night. Remember?"

Salty tears stung her eyes. How could she give a gift when there was no wedding to be had? All the dreams she had stored up these many months had disappeared, to be replaced by emptiness and sorrow. She sniffed and mumbled, "You promised me a wedding, not some legal ceremony in an office."

Keith stared at her dejected form for a moment before padding across the hardwood floors and kneeling down next to her chair. "Gail, please don't be upset. I wish there was some way I could convince you that we did the right thing."

"I just wish I was better prepared for all this. I wish I hadn't set my sights so high on having a nice wedding. I wish you'd told me earlier about your plans to elope before I went around town with Mother, trying on dresses and eating wedding cake." Her voice began to choke with emotion.

Keith took off his glasses and drew his fingers across his eyelids. "Well, things kind of came up while you were visiting your sister in Boston. There was no way I could tell you any sooner. This is the only way I could think of to avoid family interference and get on with our lives." He tossed the glasses on a nearby table and nuzzled his face in her hair. "Please believe me, Gail. I love you so much. Maybe when things settle down some, we can throw a big party for your family and friends. We'll have it in a ritzy hotel somewhere, with anything you want. I'll even buy you a beautiful ball gown to make up for the wedding dress. You'll look like a queen." He began to nibble on her earlobe.

Gail giggled. "Stop, that tickles."

"What do you say? Will that make up for all the trouble I caused you?"

She turned and gazed into his dark eyes. His arms curled around her, and she relaxed in their strength. "Well, if you think this is the right thing to do."

"I know it is. Trust me."

She melted under his warm embrace and the lips that paid hers a tender call. For the rest of the evening she forgot about weddings and receptions to enjoy their love.

&

The shrill ring of the telephone in the middle of the night

jarred them both awake. Keith fumbled for the receiver.

"Hello?" Keith sat up in a start, rubbing his weary eyes as he listened. "What? Who is this?" His fingers curled tightly around the receiver. "I'm not playing your game," he hissed. "Get off my back or you're asking for it." He tossed the receiver on the hook and buried himself in the bed once more as if to shield himself from whatever lay in wait outside the walls of the room. Soon he felt a hand shake the quilt and a whisper drifted down from above. He peeled back the cover to find Gail staring at him.

"Who was that on the phone, Keith?"

"Just a prank call. Don't worry about it."

"You tell me not to worry, but I am right now. You knew that person on the phone, didn't you? What did they want?"

Keith only buried himself beneath the quilt. "I said not to worry about it."

"Keith, please don't do this to me," Gail begged, pulling the quilt away from his face. "Don't shut me out now that we've made love and everything. I–I don't know what's going on with us. You always seemed so transparent in the past, but now I don't know. It's like there're walls between us. First, it's the secrets about your family, and now it's a mystery call. Please tell me what's going on."

Her pleading voice pulled a cord in his heart. Once more, he pushed away the quilt, took her trembling form into his arms, and cradled her close to his chest. His hand gently pushed back the curls from her face. "Shhh, it's going to be all right. Trust me."

"You tell me to trust you," Gail mumbled, pressing her face into his shoulder, "but I don't know why I should. . . ."

"Gail, Gail," he murmured, "I wanted to spare you all this. I really did. I guess I just loved you too much to let you go." He tipped back her chin, staring into brown eyes that appeared so vulnerable and afraid. He kissed her gently. Only when her tears glazed his cheek did he realize the mistake he'd made. *I should have let you go when I could have, for your own good,* he thought. *That would have been a true act of love. But I was selfish and now it's too late.*

A loud knock suddenly sounded on the door. Keith hugged Gail close to him. Again came the thump of a fist, rattling the door on its hinges. He jumped to his feet and raced to the window, searching for an exit from the room. A quick scan of the situation told him the window of the room was far too high. . . . There was no escape. He frantically searched for another idea.

"Get dressed quick," Keith whispered hoarsely. He then took Gail by the arm and shoved her to the floor. "Now, get under the bed and don't make a sound!"

"B–but, Keith, what's going on?"

"Do as I say! And keep quiet."

Gail crawled into the tight space, wedging herself between the bed and the hard floor just as the lock to the door clicked and the door swung open. Two men sauntered in. One of them pocketed a nail file.

"What do you think you're doing?" Keith demanded.

Grant's thick voice blanketed the room. "I'm sorry to disturb you, but have you forgotten about the appointment with your father?" His dark eyes swept Keith as a tiny smile hovered in the crook of his mouth.

"I don't know what you're talking about. Now get out of here!"

"I'm afraid you did make an appointment, and as I said on the phone, I intend to have you keep it."

"You're developing a big nose for trouble, pal," Keith snapped. "I told you the other day to get lost. Guess you don't understand English."

The other man began kicking over suitcases and scattering

personal belongings as he searched the room.

"Both of you get out of here right now, or I'll—"

"Call the police?" Grant interrupted. He snickered. "That would prove interesting. By all means, go ahead. In the meantime, where is your bride this evening?"

"That's none of your business."

Grant sighed and shook his head. "You really are making things difficult. I have a job to do. Your father specifically wanted to meet this fiancée. . .or wife, I should say. Now must I punish the boss's disobedient son for refusing direct orders?"

"Who are you kidding? You can't lay a finger on me and you know it."

"But there are other ways to convince you, wouldn't you say?" At that very moment, Gail was dragged out from underneath the bed by Grant's accomplice. Her enormous eyes appeared like the dark circles of a raccoon's on her pale face. She fell into Keith's arms, shaking like a tree limb in the breeze and heaving with every breath. Keith glanced over the curly ringlets of her hair to see the spark of challenge in Grant's dark eyes. He knew the man was capable of anything if he felt deterred in his work. With great reluctance, Keith ordered Gail to pack.

"But Keith, w-where are we going?"

"Just do it, Gail. Now."

She obeyed with a sniff as the two men watched her place a few meager belongings into a suitcase. Keith threw his own clothes into another bag before tossing it hard into Grant's stomach. "Here," he snorted. "Do something useful and be our bellboy. Just don't expect a tip."

"I will receive my tip after I deliver you and your bride safely to your father."

"I'm sure you will. Just like the postman. Must be a hard life."

"I rather enjoy it. The work proves quite entertaining, chasing a belligerent son from town to town. For one who doesn't wish to be followed, you don't cover your tracks well at all."

"I'm not slick like you. I intend to run my life the way I choose. I don't care who sees it."

"Unfortunately, you will have to convince your father of your new independence, won't you?" Grant began to chuckle. "That won't be easy, I can assure you."

Keith opened his mouth to counter the statement, but finding no suitable words, he clamped his mouth shut and turned away.

❧

Gail wanted to scream and cry, but fear kept the emotions bottled up within her as she followed Keith and the two men into an awaiting car. Questions assailed her mind as she cowered in the back seat, her hands clinging to Keith's arm for strength. *Who are these men? How do they know Keith? Where are they taking us in the middle of the night?* She tried replacing the confusion with peaceful thoughts as the car took off down the lighted street, but found herself in turmoil. All her mindless ideology of the past did nothing to calm the gnawing sensations of fear that whittled away her strength. In the midst of her duress, she thought of Dorrie and her strong Christian commitment. She knew how much Dorrie relied on God during those fearful times that tested her. Without knowledge of what lay ahead, Gail could only cry out in her heart, *Help me, God! I don't know what's happening, but I know You do. Please, help me.*

Despite her fear, Gail soon drifted off into a restless sleep as Keith's hand gently caressed her curly hair. The two men in the front seat did nothing but gaze out the car windows. Occasionally Grant's eyes would survey them in the rearview mirror. Once or twice he opened his mouth as if to say something, but he did not.

After a trip of some ninety minutes' duration, the car slowed before a large gate and a security phone. The abrupt change in motion sent Gail yawning and rubbing her eyes in confusion. "Where are we?" she asked as the strange man behind the wheel spoke swiftly into the phone at the gate.

Keith remained silent. The gate swung open, allowing them entrance into the estate of his father. As a youngster, he used to pride himself in the family wealth, often bragging to playmates about the large white gate and security phone that blocked all but important guests from visiting. Such thoughts of money and personal esteem were revulsive to him as he watched Gail try to understand what was happening to her.

"Home sweet home," Grant mumbled, climbing out to open their car door.

Gail followed the men through the wide doors of the home and into a beautiful foyer with a dazzling chandelier and large oval window in the rear hallway. "Where are we?" she whispered again to Keith as she beheld the finery of the home. She watched with anxiety when one of the men gestured for Keith to follow while the other tried to escort her into a separate room. Her fingers dug into Keith's arm. "No, I'm not going. Keith, please don't let them take me away from you! Please let me stay with you!"

Keith turned about with his hands inside his jeans pockets, calm and composed in the midst of the sumptuous surroundings. His reaction to this strange situation unnerved her. "It's all right, Gail. We're home."

"Home? This is your home?"

He nodded toward the sitting room. "Right. So just go in there for a bit and wait for me. I'll come back for you."

"I don't understand." Her confusion increased as she was

escorted into an elegantly appointed sitting room and the door locked behind her. Her hands trembled as she tried to sit on a sofa; she soon found herself pacing instead. After a time, the decorations in the room beckoned her to investigate. A shelving unit displayed various artifacts from around the world, including tusks, pottery, sculptures, and weaving. On the opposite wall hung a family portrait in a gilded frame. Gail ventured forward to examine the painting. The mother and father sat in armchairs with their two sons standing proudly beside them. The mother was plump yet stately, with rosy cheeks and brown hair. The father wore a huge mustache that draped across his face. Upon closer inspection, she noted that one of the youths in the painting looked something like Keith, with dark hair and eyes and a mischievous smile. The painting was dated 1985. An engraved brass plate read, "The Costello Family."

"The Costello family?" she whispered, shaking her head. Next she inspected the many artifacts lining the shelves. Each item had its own label and serial number. Someone in the family had traveled far and wide to obtain a collection of curiosities from around the globe, then had taken pains to identify and number each piece. Gail shook her head in wonderment. Could all this really belong to Keith's family? If so, why did he choose to conceal this life from her?

The door suddenly burst open, startling her. One of the men who had driven Keith and Gail to this mysterious place now waved his hand. Gail walked along the wooden flooring that creaked ominously beneath her footsteps, until she entered a large library. The odor of tobacco mixed with alcohol permeated the air. Before her sat Keith and a distinguished-looking gentleman with salt and pepper hair, and sporting a long mustache with curled tips. She drew in a sharp breath. *The man in the painting!*

The older man smiled congenially and pointed out a seat for her with the stub of a cigar. "Come sit down, young lady. I know you have had quite an extraordinary day."

Gail sent a questioning look in Keith's direction. His eyes remained fixed on the books lining the shelves.

"I hear that you two were married today by a justice of the peace."

Gail twisted the rings on her left hand with trembling fingers, wondering why she had ever agreed to Keith's proposal.

The man shifted in his leather chair. "Come now, there's no reason to be afraid. I deeply apologize if the two bodyguards who escorted you here were anything less than cordial. When I discovered my son had not arrived for his scheduled meeting, I worried for his safety and sent my men out to find him. Of course, I did not realize you were married."

Gail relaxed a bit after hearing this explanation. *So this man is Keith's father.* She glanced around the room. *He's richer than King Midas if he employs bodyguards and lives like this.* Gail jumped at the thought of wealth. She squared her shoulders and crossed her legs, trying to appear like a regal daughter-in-law. "Oh, that's all right, sir. I understand now. At the time, it was a little scary."

The man smiled before rekindling his cigar with a match. He puffed for a time, flicked the ash into a tray, then remarked, "I was sorry to hear you did not choose to proceed with a wedding. I'm sure it would have been a glorious affair."

"Yes, well. . ." Gail paused, a flush coming to her face when she recalled earlier being concerned that the patriarch of the family might not wish her to be his new daughter-in-law. "I know I'm not what you all thought I would be and everything. . . . I mean, I'm not from a very noteworthy family. We're just ordinary people, you see, and. . ." She paused when Keith gave her a strange look.

"Nonsense. Notoriety is hardly important. You seem like a very intelligent young lady. And you're quite beautiful as well. I think my son made an excellent choice."

Gail smiled for the first time that day. She felt her confidence soar, fueled by the compliments. "Well, thank you. And you have a lovely home here." A yawn escaped and she clamped a hand over her mouth. "Oh, pardon me. I guess I'm a little tired."

"Well, it is the middle of the night. The maid will show you to the guest room. I will see you again in the morning. Goodnight."

Gail rose and bid him goodnight before following the petite maid who stood waiting outside the library doors. Keith followed her up the winding stairway to a room at the end of the hall. The mere sight of the room, with a separate sitting area and private bath, left her breathless.

"Keith, you have such a wonderful home!" Gail exclaimed, bouncing up and down on the bed. "I don't know why you never told me about it. There are so many gorgeous artifacts in that sitting room, not to mention the beautiful statues and the furniture. Your family is so rich!" She slid off the bed to sink her feet into the thick carpet. "This is like living in paradise."

"Stay here awhile and you'll sing a different tune," he muttered before quickly offering her a small smile. "I suppose it is."

She straightened and looked at him expectantly. "So is this the place where you grew up?"

He nodded. "This room used to be Archie's. . .uh. . ."

"Who?"

"It was the boys' room," he said quickly. "It was changed into a guest room after we moved out."

Gail wrinkled her face in confusion. "We? You mean you have a brother?"

A strange expression swept across Keith's face. He rubbed his hands together and shuffled his feet in agitation. "Yeah, I had a brother."

"Where is he? I'd love to meet him. I bet you two squabbled a lot when you were kids, huh? You wouldn't believe the fights Dorrie and I used to have when we were little. When my parents first lived in a small apartment we had to share a bedroom, and wow, that's when the fireworks began. She wanted things done one way and I wanted them another. And Dorrie is a very messy person. I liked things neat and orderly, but you always knew when Dorrie had come through—it was like a tornado hit the room or something."

Keith's feet continued to shuffle in response to her lively chatter. "Look, Pop and I need to talk for a while. I'll be in later. Go ahead and get some sleep."

"All right."

They kissed quickly before Keith walked out of the room and stumbled down the stairs. He burst into the library where his father stood, perusing a book. "Why did you do this, Pop? Why did you send those two punks to drag us here in the middle of the night? You scared Gail half to death. Now she'll start questioning everything."

He closed the book with a thump. "Highly unlikely. You saw the look on her face. She believes an overprotective father only wanted to find his lost son. I'm thankful you at least picked yourself a naive girl without a brain."

Keith bristled. He felt his fist clench; he fought to relax. "Pop, why don't you just leave us alone and let us live our lives in peace. I'm not involved with the business anymore. You're getting along just fine without me."

His father picked up a fresh cigar from the humidor and

ran it along his mustache, inhaling the fragrance of the tobacco. "That's where you're wrong, Quin. I need you, and soon." He took up a match and lit it. "Grant has informed me that your new wife has a sister living in Boston. It works out perfectly with my plans."

Keith's eyes widened in alarm.

"I need you to go to Boston very soon to check on some business for me. Having family in the vicinity will give you an excellent reason to be in the area."

"I told you I don't want to be involved anymore."

His father's eyes glinted like a predator in the darkness as he puffed on the cigar. "You have no choice in the matter. You're in this with me. You always have been and always will be. Don't think for a moment you won't be recognized in New York, San Francisco, Chicago, or half a dozen other cities where we've conducted business. Your name's known in the inner circles, just like mine."

"It's been over a year since I've done anything significant. And about my name—you might as well know that I'm going by a new alias. Gail knows me as Keith Hampton, not Quintin Costello. So don't use my real name while she's here."

The older Costello cracked a smile and gestured at Keith's eyeglasses with his cigar. "And I assume those glasses you wear are to further conceal your identity. You think just like your father. You are crafty, but also adept at handling my affairs." He stepped closer, his voice softening. "Quintin, I need you. You're my heir. You must know what to do with the business if something ever happens to me."

"Pop, I don't intend to—"

His father held up a hand, silencing him. "Don't even say it. You are my only heir, with both your mother and Archie gone." He choked as he added, "You're all I have left in the world besides this estate, which is far too big for an old man like me."

"Pop. . . ," he began, knowing it was senseless to argue. His father would only continue in his tactic of persuasion by dredging up the pain he carried for the dissolution of his family. He would then wave his hand, while acknowledging his vast holdings, and claim that he wanted his only son to have his inheritance.

"Don't make me have to spell it out for you," his father continued. "We're both in this for the duration. You made a commitment to remain by my side."

"Yeah, but it's different now, Pop. I'm married. I have new responsibilities."

"I know you're married, much to my displeasure. I warned you about the consequences. I won't let some marriage certificate change what we have agreed to."

"But it does!" Keith retorted, pacing before the sullen master of the household. "Everything has changed. I don't want Gail involved in any of this."

"She doesn't have to be. Keep her out of it. You know how."

Keith paused before his father. "You mean live a lie. You did the same thing with Mother, and look what happened to her."

A pained expression crossed the man's face. He spat out the cigar into an ash tray. Gnarled fingers groped for the shot glass brimming with brandy that he threw down his throat. "You're blaming me again for that. I've told you time and time again I had nothing to do with it."

"But you drove her to it, Pop. She was never happy. She knew things were going on right underneath her nose. Then after Archie died, she couldn't take it anymore and she. . . ," Keith paused, unable to voice the consequence of his mother's depression. All the family's riches and lavish lifestyle were not enough to keep her in the land of the living.

His hand flicked away a sudden tear escaping down his cheek. "Anyway, I won't have the same thing happening to Gail. She thinks my mother is alive and well and everything in the family is cool. I don't want her to know what drove Mother over the brink."

He strode out of the library, ignoring the assortment of faces peeking out from various recesses within the grand hallway. His father's spies lurked everywhere, eavesdropping on the discussion. The Costello household was a grand avenue for the corrupt who were eager to make fast money by accommodating Keith's father. Gazing about at the luxurious surroundings, Keith felt sick to his stomach. Something would have to give in all this—but what, he didn't know. All he knew for sure was that he could not have Gail caught in the middle.

Keith peeked in the guest room and found Gail asleep. He stroked her soft cheek with his finger. It would be difficult to hide the circumstances of his family's wealth from someone as curious as Gail. Undoubtedly, she would find out everything. And if he tried to shield her from it, what then? He bit his lip, recalling his mother's reaction to the family secrets. He could not bear to see Gail driven off the same precipice that had claimed his mother. He closed his eyes, perplexed about what to do in the days ahead.

six

Gail awoke the next morning to find her clothes pressed and laid out for her on a nearby chair. Next to her, the bed was still made up. She frowned, wondering where Keith had spent the night. As she climbed out of bed, a delicious fragrance greeted her. A beautiful arrangement of long-stemmed red roses in a cut-glass vase sat on the dresser. The heavenly aroma filled her nostrils as she skipped over to the adjoining bath to take a shower.

Despite the terrifying events of the previous evening, it thrilled her to be in the midst of such luxury. She couldn't understand why Keith disliked the beautiful surroundings. Perhaps such wealth lost its allure after a lifetime of exposure to it. For Gail, who had lived her entire life in low- to middle-income housing, the elegance was a treat. As the soothing spray of the shower washed away the anxieties of yesterday, she reminded herself to be bright and cheerful so Keith's father and mother would accept her. She didn't want to do anything that might irritate them, especially knowing that she had married into their wealth.

Scrubbing her arms with a sponge, she suddenly realized that Keith's purchase of ten-thousand-dollar wedding bands did not seem extravagant now that the money situation had become clear. Many times she had dreamt of walking into a store and buying the most expensive item on the shelf. She grew tired of always having to settle for cheap imitations. She stopped scrubbing and smiled. Why, now she could have anything she wanted! She had married into wealth! Gail closed her eyes as the water sprayed her face, imagining the fancy house she and Keith would buy, complete with an in-ground swimming pool and a tennis court. She would hire a personal maid and have her own hair styling salon right inside the house.

Gail stepped out of the shower and quickly toweled herself dry. Today she must look and feel her best. She would put on plenty of makeup to hide the flaws in her skin, and eye shadow to highlight the color of her irises. Sighing in dismay at her wardrobe, she wished she had brought along fancier outfits. After spending about an hour pampering herself and carefully making up her face, Gail opened the door and peeked into the hall. She tiptoed carefully to the top of the stairs. The chandelier in the hallway glimmered as she walked down each step, glancing around the banister for Keith. The maid, dressed in a standard black uniform and white apron, came out into the foyer and offered her a smile.

"Good morning, Miss. Breakfast will be served on the patio. If you will follow me."

Breakfast on the patio! Gail thought. *How lovely.* She walked through glass doors and out onto a brick patio decorated with white wicker furniture. Flowers in large earthen pots bloomed in abundance. Beyond the patio was an in-ground pool filled with crystal blue waters, and a cabana for changing. *Just like the home of a famous movie star,* she thought dreamily, sitting down in one of the wicker chairs. The entire back yard was fenced with black wrought iron that, in places, was covered by thick vines. Birds darted above her, chirping their merry morning songs.

"Good morning," a deep voice addressed her. She turned to see Keith and his father walk out to the patio; they drew up wicker chairs opposite her. "And how was your night?" asked Keith's father.

"Oh, just fine, sir," Gail said, offering the family patriarch her best smile. Glancing over in Keith's direction, she noticed the dark circles under his eyes and the worry lines etched in a distinct pattern around his mouth. It was apparent he had slept poorly. She wondered again where he had spent the night before pushing the thought aside. "I noticed your lovely pool. Do you swim a lot in it, Mr. Hampton?"

"I enjoy a dip now and then. It's refreshing to take a swim when the temperature rises in the afternoon. Perhaps you would like a swim while you are here?"

Gail's eyes sparkled. "I would love it!" Again her eyes darted over to Keith, who sat slumped in his chair with his chin resting in his hand.

Soon the maid arrived to serve breakfast. Bowls filled with fresh fruit and plump blueberry muffins caused Gail to salivate in anticipation. "Coffee?" the woman asked, holding up the crystal pot.

"Oh yes, please. Keith was telling me he can drink coffee any time of day and it has no effect on him."

The father glanced at his son. "Well, he must have inherited the trait from me." He cleared his throat. "In fact, we are very much alike in many respects."

Gail sipped the steaming coffee before asking, "Is your mother sleeping in, Keith?"

At this, Keith jumped as though he'd been stung by a bee. "No. She, uh. . .she. . ."

"She's out of town on business, my dear," the father interrupted. "I'm deeply sorry she isn't here to greet her new daughter-in-law. I'm sure she would find you absolutely delightful."

"I'm sorry, too. What does she do?"

"Oh, she's a. . .um, fashion consultant. Why, I'm certain that at this very moment she is enjoying breakfast at a cafe in New

York City." He chuckled as he raised his china coffee cup.

Keith only bobbed his knees back and forth while looking off in the direction of the high iron fencing surrounding the property.

"Keith mentioned he had a brother, too. Does he live nearby?"

Both father and son exchanged glances before the father said softly, "He was killed in a dreadful accident, my dear."

Gail immediately put down her coffee cup to stare at Keith. "Oh, I'm so sorry. I didn't know."

"That's quite all right. It was a terrible tragedy. He was driving late one night and lost control of his car. He hit a tree head on."

Gail tried reaching for Keith's hand across the table, but he had tucked his hands beneath his arms as if to shield himself. "Keith, I'm sorry. Here I rambled on about Dorrie last night without even thinking. That was really insensitive of me."

"Don't worry about it, Gail," he said quietly. "You didn't know. It's just, well, hard to talk about."

"Let's switch to another topic, shall we?" his father quickly interjected. "I'm glad you both are here together. I wanted to inform you of a decision I've reached concerning a wedding gift. Quin. . .uh, Keith tells me he would like to take you on an extended honeymoon, young lady. So I've decided to pay all the expenses as my wedding gift to the both of you. Wherever you decide to go, it's on me."

Gail's eyes widened in astonishment. "Really? That sounds wonderful; thank you!"

"You're quite welcome. Discuss it and I will have my travel agency make all the arrangements. In fact, I will even have the butler, Charles, locate some of those travel brochures we keep in a file drawer in the office. Look them over at your leisure."

Gail was about to announce a desire of going to Paris or

Rome when Keith announced in a sharp voice, "I already told Gail we're going to the Caribbean."

"But Keith, you heard your father. He said anywhere we want! That means Europe too, doesn't it?"

The father smiled before reaching into the pocket of his jacket to pull out a cigar. "That's right. Europe, a Mediterranean cruise, Hong Kong, wherever you choose."

"You see? How can we pass up this opportunity? If we can't have a wedding, then at least we can have a beautiful honeymoon."

She was perplexed to see Keith absently pull apart a muffin until it was no more than a mass of crumbs on his plate. He downed his coffee in several gulps before excusing himself to wander off on his own.

&

Anxiety had assailed Keith as he'd watched the cool manipulation of Anton Costello at work on the love of his life. He remembered the countless days and nights when his father had employed the same tactics on his mother—kind words, smiles, gifts, trips—all the while concealing the true business dealings of the family. Now, with Gail exposed to similar techniques, Keith understood all too well the lies his mother had endured for years. During that time, he had worshiped his father, who provided the family with everything they desired. No one questioned what Anton Costello did or with whom he associated. Instead, family members became involved in their own activities.

Archie, the older of the two Costello sons, was studious and thoughtful—but a weakling, his father would sometimes say with a sneer. Yet Archie found favor with their mother, Treva, who liked his quiet ways. Quintin, or Keith, as he now addressed himself, was the more adventuresome of the two. His father loved him for that, and found him dependable and trustworthy with the company secrets. When Keith grew older, he remained constantly by his father's side, intrigued by the danger attending the business. His mind assimilated with ease any information his father cared to share. Nothing excited him more than traveling with his father or the other men to the major cities, arranging meetings with their contacts, finding out about shipments, and collecting goods to sell for profit. Most of all, he enjoyed the challenge of outwitting the law enforcement agencies that sought to subdue them.

As the business expanded into major cities throughout the United States, his father hired on new people to help, including Grant, who was well known in the circles of corruption for his organizational skills and his ability to spy on adversaries. Keith and Grant immediately locked horns, for Keith felt the man eroded Keith's influence within the business. At about the same time, his older brother, Archie, began complaining about all the unlawful activity. He had recently undergone a religious experience—a "brainwashing by lunatics," as Keith called the conversion. Those in the business watched with apprehension as Archie began warning his father to change his ways or reconcile himself with the authorities. The threat alarmed everyone, especially Grant, who had settled into the business well and looked forward to a promotion within the chain of command.

Then one night the family received the disturbing news of Archie's death in an automobile accident. The vehicle had been found against a tree with the front end smashed as though a giant fist had dealt the death blow. Archie had perished instantly. His death sent Keith's mother into a deep depression; she refused to leave her room for days on end. Keith delved into the workings of the business to escape the pain. A few months after Archie's funeral, he and his father left on an extended trip to Europe, leaving his mother in the care of friends. When they arrived home, they were met with more tragedy; Treva Costello had overdosed on a deadly combination of sedatives and alcohol and now fought for life in the intensive care unit of Albany Medical Center. Keith visited his mother only once while she was there. The tubes in her arms and neck sickened him. After several days of struggle the troubled woman died, grieving over the loss of her eldest son and her life in general.

Keith brushed away a stray tear as he recalled her funeral, held under an overcast sky. Anton Costello had been all business in response to his wife's death and never mourned, as far as Keith could tell. Likewise, Keith had masked the effects of his own grief until just recently, when he began sensing the loss of his mother. Hearing Gail's incessant chatter about her family, it pained him that his mother was no longer alive to share in his life. There were only the harsh demands of a headstrong father who insisted that Keith remain in the business, despite his marriage to Gail.

The soft touch of a hand on his arm sent Keith whirling around to find Gail staring at him, an inquisitive look in her brown eyes. When she inquired about his moodiness, a wall of solid stone rose up within him.

"Guess it's hard remembering Archie and all," Keith mumbled.

Gail leaned her curly head against his chest. He could not help but run his fingers through her hair. The gesture brought comfort to his troubled soul.

"I wish I hadn't talked so much about Dorrie last night."

"It's okay," he said. "Dorrie's your sister."

"Yes, but—"

"Hey, I mean it. After the honeymoon is over, we'll make a trip to Boston and visit her."

"I know she'll like you. And I bet you'll get along great

with her husband, Mick. He's built like you—broad shoul-dered with big muscles." Gail ran a finger across a rippling bicep before slipping her hand around his upper arm. "He's athletic, too, but really into religion, like Dorrie. He teaches biology at a middle school, then on weekends he does some pretty dangerous stuff."

Keith was suddenly riveted. "What dangerous stuff?"

"You wouldn't believe it." They walked arm in arm until they reached the far side of the pool. Gail knelt down to pluck out a few stray leaves floating in the warm water. "He works with the gangs right in the heart of Boston. I don't know how he does it. I would be scared stiff."

Keith's eyes widened as he glanced quickly toward the patio to find that his father had left. He knelt beside Gail as she trailed her fingers in the water. "What do you mean he works with the gangs? What does he do?"

"Oh, he helps run a soup kitchen. Then he goes out on the street and talks to gang members about God. Dorrie doesn't want him doing it anymore. She's afraid he'll end up like his father."

"What happened to his father?"

"Some gang leader shot him in the back of the head. Mick's father used to work with a gang called the Vultures. One day they just shot him, in an alley. Now he lives in a nursing home because he can't do anything for himself. I've even visited him there. He can't talk or feed himself. Every day the nurses have to dress him and wheel him around. It's really sad. The only good thing is that he does know what's going on. Mick and Dorrie talk to him all the time. He even smiled once when they brought in my little nephew, Jamie, for a visit."

Keith listened carefully as he piled up a mound of white stones that bordered the pool. "And this all happened in Boston?"

She nodded.

"When?"

"About six years ago. It was terrible. I can't believe Mick still wants to go out there and talk to that gang after what they did to his father. He's crazy to take such risks." She came and nuzzled her head against his chest. Instinctively, Keith wrapped his arms around her. "That's why I'm so glad you're not involved with anything dangerous. I simply couldn't take it."

A strange sensation overcame him. He released her and rose to his feet. "Say, let's get our minds off gangs and violence and have a look at those travel brochures, shall we?"

Gail flashed him a look of surprise. "Does this mean I get to choose someplace other than the Caribbean for our honeymoon?"

Keith nodded, watching her eyes light up in excitement. "You heard Pop. It's on him. Might as well take him up on his generosity—for now, anyway."

"Oh, goody!" she sighed in delight, skipping alongside him like a young child who had been given a grand Christmas present. "I can't wait!"

Keith hardly felt like celebrating as his mind buzzed with the information concerning Gail's brother-in-law in Boston. He made up his mind to speak with his father about it as soon as he engaged Gail's interest in the travel brochures.

⁂

Anton Costello sat calmly at his large mahogany desk, a cigar smoking away in the ash tray. Keith entered and sat in one of the high-back leather chairs. His father glanced up upon his arrival and offered a small smile. "Well, have you decided where you would like to go for your honeymoon?"

"Gail is looking over the brochures right now."

"And has she found anything interesting?"

"Everything interests Gail. She'll find it hard to reach a decision." Keith leaned over with his hands clasped together and his elbows resting on his knees. "Pop, I've got something important to tell you."

"Yes, what is it?" Costello asked carelessly, shuffling through the stack of papers littering his desk.

"I just found out something I think you should know. Gail was telling me about her sister and brother-in-law who live in Boston. She told me her brother-in-law's father, who's one of those street preachers, was shot six years ago; he was involved with a gang in Boston."

Keith's father raised his bushy gray eyebrows to acknowledge Keith's concerned face.

"It seems to me I recall some kind of fiasco back about that time in Boston," Keith continued. "It was a gang called the Vandals or something."

"The *Vultures,*" his father corrected, rattling papers as if in an effort to drown out the discussion. "What of it, Quintin?"

"Well, correct me if I'm wrong, but I remember you putting someone on the hit list about that same time—someone who was interfering with the gang and the business and who needed to be dealt with. Was it that street preacher?"

Anton Costello shrugged indifferently. "I don't keep track of incidents that took place more than five years ago. If the man in question had his nose in our business, it's entirely possible that we put him on the list."

Keith shot out of his seat. "Pop, do you realize what you're saying? One of your people shot a member of Gail's extended family!"

"Calm down, Quintin, and take a seat." He pointed to the chair with the tip of his cigar before plugging it back into his mouth.

"No, I'm not going to sit. Think what you have done to

Gail's family! All the heartache, the loss of a loved one. . . ."

Costello stared with frosty eyes. "Quintin, you of all people should know that when someone begins to infiltrate our organization, he must be silenced or we risk discovery." He paused, flicking the ash from his cigar before returning it to his mouth. "Yes, I do vaguely recall the incident. There was some unknown individual—I believe he *was* a street preacher, now that you mention it—who had infiltrated the Vultures gang. He started asking all the wrong questions. He needed to be silenced before he leaked vital information to the police. I believe the gang leader himself took the full rap for the shooting." He added with pride, "Fortunately, none of my men were implicated in the deed. We were very careful."

Keith stared at his father. The man sitting before him was no longer a human being but a block of hard flesh, frozen by years of relentless criminal activity. "I don't believe you're actually saying this! An innocent man is a vegetable in some nursing home because one of your men plugged a bullet into his brain, and all you can do is boast about not being caught?"

Costello rose, snarling, "That preacher was no innocent man, let me tell you. He was a danger to our entire operation in Boston! If he had gone to the cops, you and I would both be rusting behind bars the rest of our lives." He took out the cigar and pointed it at Keith like a weapon. "If I were you, I'd put a stop right now to this lovesick, mercy routine you're infected with and face the hard facts. We're here to run a business and make a profit. Period."

Keith began to pace before the desk. "I don't want any part of this. I mean it. I'm through."

"It's too late to back out now. You're too involved. Don't think for a moment you won't go down with the rest of us if you start getting soft on me. Just remember that everything about you is known on every street corner of every major city. A new name or a pair of glasses won't protect you if any of this leaks out. You know full well that when someone on the outside knows too much, he must be disposed of, plain and simple." Costello stuffed the cigar back into his mouth and sat down.

Keith stared hard at his father. "So tell me, Pop, did this hit list of yours also include family members? Like Archie, maybe? Or Mother?"

The older man's face went white as he spat out the cigar. "Are you out of your mind? How dare you even suggest such a thing!"

Keith spun around and headed for the door.

"Quintin, come back here! I'm not finished with you!"

Keith's hand rested on the doorknob. "Yes, you are. I'm finished with this whole rotten thing. Gail and I will be leaving shortly on that glorious honeymoon you promised us. From now on, you just leave us alone." He left with the door slamming behind him, refusing to acknowledge the shadowy figure standing in a dark recess of the hallway, staring with piercing black eyes.

seven

When Gail and Keith arrived back in Westchester County, they were besieged with questions from Gail's parents regarding the hasty marriage performed by the justice of the peace. Huge tears gathered in Gail's mother's eyes as she pulled out the wedding dress she had purchased during their absence. Her father sat in a recliner inside the family room, shaking his head in dismay.

"I don't know if I can return this now," Mother lamented to Gail, as a finger traced the delicately curved neckline and the fancy beadwork on the bodice of the dress. "This was supposed to be a surprise. I was going to have you try it on and arrange for all the necessary alterations." She stared unhappily at Gail and then Keith. "I don't understand why you eloped after all the plans we'd made."

"It's kind of hard to explain," Gail began with a sideways glance at Keith, hoping for some support. He just stood there, silent, with his hands jammed in his pockets. "Keith's family. . .well. . ."

"I talked Gail into it," Keith finally told them. "I thought it would be the best thing to do, considering my family situation."

Gail's father shot him a look that could have melted ice. "And what's that supposed to mean, young man? We gave our permission for you to marry our daughter on the assumption that there would be a wedding ceremony in a church, officiated by an ordained minister. I cannot understand why you decided to elope."

Her mother continued to sniff and dab her eyes with a tissue.

"All the plans. . .everything ruined!"

Her father pointed to the sofa, urging Gail and Keith to sit. "Let's just talk about this rationally, without all the emotion." When they were seated, he continued. "So what is it about your family that is so worrisome, young man?"

"Dad, they're rich," Gail interrupted. "I mean filthy rich, with a mansion, an in-ground pool, a fancy cabana, the works. I think Keith was afraid I wouldn't be accepted into his wealthy family. He didn't want them saying no."

"I love your daughter, sir," Keith added. "I, well, I couldn't take the chance that my family might interfere with our wedding plans. I. . .I didn't want them spoiling it. Eloping seemed the only logical alternative."

"I see," Gail's father said quietly. "So your parents don't like the idea of their rich son marrying the daughter of a blue collar worker, is that it?"

"No, sir, that's not it at all," Keith answered in all earnestness. "I mean, now that my father has met Gail, he likes her very much."

"But you pushed my Gail into a commitment before she was ready," Gail's mother added, the bitterness lacing her voice. "You must have known how much this wedding means to her and the rest of our family."

"I do now," he admitted meekly, staring down at his sneakers.

The Sheltons exchanged rueful glances, trying to make sense of it all. "Well, what's done is done," her father finally said. "However, I hope you will at least consider having a decent marriage ceremony in a church, even if you are legally married under the law."

"Well, maybe after the honeymoon, Dad," Gail said. "We're leaving in just a few days."

"A few days!" her mother moaned. "Where?"

Gail squeezed Keith's hand in anticipation. "Oh, we're

going to take a fabulous ten-day tour of Europe. It'll be simply wonderful! London, Paris, Stockholm, Amsterdam, and there will be ritzy hotels, fabulous restaurants, and the best shopping in the world! Keith's father offered to pay all the expenses as a wedding gift to us."

Keith aimed a weak smile toward Gail's parents, who only stared at him in disdain. Their eyes burrowed into him as if attempting to uncover his real intentions. At times, Keith found himself questioning his own motive. He vowed that all the secrecy was out of love and a concern for Gail, yet the more he tried to hide the truth about the Costello family from the curious people in his midst, the more he found himself tumbling into a deep pit. Right now there was nothing else he could do; lies and deception seemed to be the only way to protect Gail and her family. After the recent conversation with his father, he knew no one, not even Gail, would be safe if she were to discover the truth behind the Costello empire.

Keith straightened in his seat and managed another lopsided smile to hide the turmoil brewing within him. "After all I put Gail through, I thought she would enjoy a relaxing trip to Europe. But once we return, we should have that ceremony you've suggested, Mr. Shelton. I can't promise my family's participation, though. They do whatever they please."

"Well, I suppose I will have to be happy with that," he answered, rising slowly to his feet to offer Keith a handshake. "I only wish you two had confided in us."

"I'm sorry, Dad," Gail told him, running to give him a hug. "Please don't be angry with us. I'm happy, really I am."

"We're not angry," he said, stealing a quick glance at his wife. "We're just disappointed that we couldn't share in your special union."

Both Keith and Gail were thankful when the discussion ended with a minimal amount of conflict. Although there were sad faces, accompanied by a few harsh words, the Sheltons appeared ready to accept the marriage and offer whatever assistance they could to help the newlyweds adjust to their new life.

That afternoon, while her mother offered Gail suggestions concerning her wardrobe for the upcoming honeymoon, Keith ventured downtown to a travel agency to confirm the itinerary for the trip. Once inside, he settled into a chair before a huge desk. On the other side of the desk sat a young girl with red hair and bulky jewelry. She gave him a bright smile as she tapped her red-painted fingernails on a keyboard, entering the information he gave to her.

"Yes, Mr. Hampton, you and your wife are confirmed for Flight 102 leaving for Paris, France on the fifteenth. Departure time is 7:05 P.M. from JFK. I have your hotel reservations right here, as well as train tickets for your other destinations in Europe."

Keith tapped his fingers on the desk while waiting for the printer to spit out the information A thought suddenly crossed his mind. He leaned over and asked if a Grant Sotari was also scheduled for the flight.

The girl typed in the name and waited a minute or two as the computer scanned the passenger list. "No, sir, I don't see his name listed."

Keith thought for another minute, then said, "Try the name Leon Fish."

The girl raised her eyebrows. "Leon Fish? Are you kidding? What kind of a name is that?"

"Just try it, please."

She shrugged and typed in the name. "I can't imagine being born with a name like that. . . . Well, what do you know; there is a Leon Fish on the cabin passenger list."

Keith's heart began to race. He rose to his feet and ran

fingers through his hair. *So Grant is going as I suspected he would. That means he'll be tracking us every minute of the trip. Somehow I have to throw him off, but how?* He searched his mind for an idea until his eyes fell on a glossy brochure lying on the desk. He picked it up. "What's this?"

"Oh, the customer who was here before you just booked a weekend trip to Lake Louise next month."

"Lake Louise?"

"Why yes, in the Canadian Rockies, about a hundred miles west of Calgary in Alberta, Canada. The Olympic Winter Games were held in Calgary a while back—I think in 1988."

Keith opened up the leaflet and briefly reviewed the hotel amenities. "Looks like a nice place."

"Oh, it is. I have relatives who've been there. That's the Chateau Lake Louise you're looking at. It's a premier hotel built on the shore of an alpine lake. The Victoria Glacier is in the background. Of course it's still a little chilly there this time of year, but the hotel itself is quite—"

"Sounds good to me. Book us a week's stay at this, uh. . . Chateau whatever."

She arched her eyebrows.

"And you fly in where?" Keith inquired.

"The nearest regional airport is in Calgary, Alberta."

"Then I want a flight to Calgary leaving on the fifteenth, first class—make it an early evening flight out of JFK."

"But excuse me," she interrupted, glancing at the itinerary, "that's the same day you're scheduled to leave for Paris, France."

"The Canada trip is for my friend, Quintin Costello," Keith said hurriedly. "He's jealous because I'm taking this whirlwind tour of Europe. Maybe a trip like this will keep him happy."

"I'm sure it will," she said, typing in the name as Keith spelled it for her.

"And put down his girlfriend. . .uh, Dorrie Shelton."

"Dorrie? Is that her real name?"

"I think so, but you never know about my friend. He gets a new girlfriend every week. Maybe after this trip he'll change his mind and finally marry this one."

"All right, then. I assume you want a rental car for them?"

Keith nodded. "The best you have available. Maximum upgrade."

"Yes, sir." After a few minutes of typing and scanning the computer readouts, she said, "I have your friend and his girl-friend scheduled to depart at six P.M. from JFK on flight 253, first class, arriving in Calgary at 9:30, but of course that's mountain time. Unfortunately, since you booked so late, the round-trip flight for two will cost the maximum list price of eleven hundred fifty-two dollars and thirty cents with tax, not counting the rental car for ground transportation and the hotel fees."

"Just total it all up and I'll pay it," Keith said. "Be sure you book a nice room at that hotel, too. Make it the honey-moon suite and maybe they'll even get hitched in time to use it. And another thing, Miss. . .?"

The girl whirled around in her seat. "Oh, I'm Darcy. Darcy Weeks."

"Ms. Weeks," he said, slipping her a hundred dollar bill from his wallet, "if some guy comes walking in here with dark hair and a pitted face, asking about these arrangements, I would prefer it if you didn't spill the beans. My friend will try every trick in the book to discover what's going on. The man's quite sly, you know. I've had a hard time keeping secrets from him. Just say you never saw me."

"Wow," Darcy exclaimed, staring at the hundred dollar bill he offered. "Why, sure! No problem."

"In fact, I'll make it two for your trouble." He added another of the bills to the one sitting in the palm of her hand. "I care about my friend, but he sure doesn't care about himself. Now print up that itinerary quickly so I can get out of here."

"Oh yes, right away." Darcy whirled around in her seat to face the computer and madly typed away as though the money had energized her fingers. Keith sat still, his thoughts churning. He knew Gail would be disappointed at the change of plans, but he must keep one step ahead of Grant in this game or lose much more than he could afford to lose.

❧

"Why do I need Dorrie's birth certificate when I already have my own passport?" Gail wanted to know as she searched a file cabinet in her father's office for the original document. "I'm so glad I decided to go ahead and get my passport a few years back."

"Just trust me, you'll need it."

Gail peered up at Keith with a perturbed expression. "I hate it when you say, 'Just trust me.' That means you're up to something, doesn't it? You're the most mysterious man in the world, Keith Hampton. It's like you're playing a game with me or something."

"Well, this really is a game of sorts. It's like Stratego. Ever play it?"

Gail shook her head.

"I'll have to show you how sometime. I used to play it a lot when I was a kid. The object of the game is to capture your opponent's flag. You hide your pieces and use them to destroy your opponent's men in order to reach his flag.

"It sounds confusing, if you ask me."

"Well, as you go step by step, you begin to reveal the pieces you have hidden from your opponent. So you might say I'm slowly revealing pieces of my strategy to you."

"Yes, but I'm not your enemy," Gail teased, her face suddenly turning serious. "At least I didn't think I was."

Keith chuckled as he wrapped an arm around her. "Of course you're not my enemy. I'm thinking of others at this moment. The only way I can capture my enemy's flag and win is to reveal as few of my men as possible at any one time."

Gail shook her head before returning to her search inside the file cabinet. "You're so confusing, Keith. I wish things could just be spelled out simply. Life is too complicated, hanging around with you."

He sighed. "I wish it wasn't so complicated. There are many decisions I've made over the course of my life that I wish I could change. Sometimes I wish I could be born all over again, and start my life fresh."

Gail laughed as she withdrew the birth certificate with Dorrie's tiny baby footprints stamped on the back. "Yeah, but you can't. We're only born once, unless you believe in reincarnation or something."

"Reincarnation," he snickered. "Yeah. For all you know, you may have eloped with a guy who once lived as an Arabian prince in another life."

Gail lifted an eyebrow. "It's a good thing Dorrie isn't around to hear you say that. She'd have a fit. The one time I mentioned reincarnation, she exploded, informing me that it was a mystic philosophy that people use so they won't have to face the day of judgment. She says that, according to the Bible, you only live once and then comes judgment before the throne of God or something." Both became silent, pondering that inadvertent mention of the Bible.

Later that evening, they enjoyed a pleasant dinner at one of their favorite restaurants. While driving back in the car, Keith picked up Gail's hand and held it in his. "I haven't mentioned this to you because of everything going on these last few days. I hope we can soon start acting like a married couple, if you know what I mean."

"I know. I've thought about it, too. I'm feeling better about everything, now that we are going on our honeymoon. I guess it's a little unnerving, being at our parents' homes." She leaned back in her seat. "Why don't we celebrate while we're on our honeymoon? Isn't that what you're supposed to do anyway?"

Keith doubted she would even want to be with him after discovering what he had done to her honeymoon plans. "Gail, I don't want to wait any longer than I have to. I've been really patient and—"

"I know you have. C'mon, though, wouldn't it be more romantic to experience love in Paris?" She giggled at the thought before resting her curly head on his shoulder.

"Paris," he echoed. *I only hope and pray you'll feel the same way about Canada.*

 za

The next day Keith decided to take a stroll around the neighborhood to sort out any remaining details before leaving for Canada. He grew edgier as the time drew near, wondering how Gail would react to their change in destination. Yet the more he thought about it, the more the plan made sense. Grant would never suspect that they would change their honeymoon destination to some Arctic region in the far north. Surely this plan would outwit his clever opponent and allow Keith and Gail a welcome breather after the recent upheaval in their lives.

As Keith rounded a corner, he spotted a figure leaning against the side of a small metal booth, casually speaking into a telephone. He darted behind a row of parked cars and crawled along the pavement until he was within earshot of the conversation.

"Yes, sir, I checked with the travel agency here in town,"

the voice said. "They are still listed as passengers on the flight to Paris this evening."

Keith's muscles tightened as he recognized Grant's voice.

"No sir, I have not seen anything out of the ordinary. Yes, we are also confirmed for the flight. However, you do realize your son will become quite belligerent once he discovers us on the trip." There was a pause. "Yes, but the idea of a bodyguard has never settled well with young Quintin." Another pause. "It will be difficult to change his mind concerning the business, but I understand the seriousness of the situation."

Through a window of the parked car Keith could see Grant's head nodding up and down as fingers fumbled in a shirt pocket for a cigarette.

"Are you certain that's what you want?" Grant asked, tucking the receiver beneath his chin as he lit a smoke. "Very well, then. I have yet to fail you, sir, as you know. I will call you from Paris when we arrive."

Keith ducked behind the auto and watched from the ground as Grant's feet shuffled to and fro. The odor of cigarette smoke floated down on him from above. After a time, the feet clad in dark shoes moved off down the street. Keith closed his eyes and heaved a sigh of relief. The conversation had confirmed one major detail; had he not changed the itinerary for the honeymoon, both Gail and he would have found themselves at the mercy of his adversary.

Keith rose to his feet and brushed off the gravel from his jeans, preparing to head back to the house when a voice stopped him dead in his tracks.

"So you also like to spy, young Costello?"

Keith jerked around in response. Grant appeared from behind the car with a sardonic grin plastered on his face. Regaining his composure, Keith said quickly, "Unfortunately, spying is a necessary evil when I hear there'll be two unwanted stowaways on board our flight to Paris tonight." He chuckled scornfully. "Really, Grant, I had no idea you were also planning a honeymoon."

Grant stood puffing on his cigarette. He blew rings of smoke into the air before he said, "Agree to remain in the business, young Costello, and I won't have to make the trip."

"Haven't you learned yet that what I do in the business is none of *your* business?"

"And haven't you learned that whatever interests your father interests me? Your father's primary concern is that your youthful presence remains within our organization. I intend to see that his wish is carried out."

"Let's discuss the options after my honeymoon, like normal, decent people." Keith slapped his forehead. "Whoops, I forgot—you're not normal, are you, Grant? In fact, you're far from normal. I always thought your primary habitation should be the exotic species exhibit at the Bronx Zoo."

Grant flicked cigarette ash on the ground before Keith's sneakers. "While you do have a sharp wit, Quin, you have no smarts. The only way one can succeed in this game is to be smart."

"I intend to succeed. I'm going to win the game by capturing your flag, buddy." He whirled, ready to saunter away.

"I would not try to challenge me or you will regret it."

Keith turned and walked backwards with confidence. "It's too late for that, bud. This is a challenge. We'll find out soon enough who has the real smarts in this game. See you in Paris." He walked briskly down the sidewalk as the other man stood calmly beside the parked car, smoking the cigarette until the butt fell to the ground and his shoe smashed it flat.

eight

"Are you finally going to tell me about this game of yours?" Gail asked as she checked her makeup in a lighted compact.

Keith's hands tightened around the wheel of the car he had rented for the trip to Kennedy Airport. He frequently glanced in his rearview mirror, looking for any sign that Grant and his associate might be following, but found nothing unusual. He made painstaking efforts to conceal their tracks by driving an out-of-the-way route to the largest international airport in the United States. He hoped the effort would pay off.

Keith braked at a stoplight. "Well, I guess I should tell you what I've decided to do before we reach the airport. You must believe that this is for your own good, Gail."

She dropped her compact inside her purse. Her lips curved downward into a frown. "I know what you're going to say. We're not going to Paris, are we?"

Keith flashed her a look of astonishment. "How did you know?"

A muscle twitched in one smooth cheek as she folded her arms and looked out the window. "Because nothing in this relationship has turned out the way I expected. The honeymoon had to be next on the list."

An uneasy Keith noticed Gail's growing agitation. How would she react when he told her their new destination? He began by gently informing her of a place he had found that was devoid of the hassles of hotel transfers and traveling through foreign lands.

"You mean you found someplace better than Europe?"

Beads of sweat gathered along the back of his neck, dampening the collar of his shirt. He steered the car onto the expressway. "Well, not exactly. Look, Gail, I'll be frank with you. Remember those two guys who came stalking us the night we eloped, then drove us to my father's home in the middle of the night?"

"How could I forget? That was the most terrifying night of my life!"

"Well, my father put the same men on the flight to Paris with us."

Gail stared at him, aghast. "Why, for goodness sake?"

"Supposedly to act as bodyguards while we are in a foreign country. But I can tell you for a fact, these aren't the kind of characters you can trust in a dark alley. Just because they work for my pop doesn't mean they're well mannered, not by any stretch of the imagination."

"So you changed the plans for the honeymoon because of them?"

"Yes, and that's why I had you locate your sister's birth certificate. You're going as your sister Dorrie, so you won't need your passport."

"And who are you going as?"

Keith flushed. "Oh, I picked a family name out of the hat. Anyway, I had to throw these two guys off track, so I arranged for an alternate destination. The girl at the travel agency highly recommended it. And I reserved the honeymoon suite. The hotel overlooks this nice lake. I'm sure you'll love it."

"But where's it at?"

"Uh. . . ," he paused, glancing once more in his rearview mirror, "well, it's in Canada."

"Canada! You mean Montreal? I've never been to Montreal. You know, they speak French in that province. I guess it would be just like going to France."

"Actually, it's in a real scenic part of the country—the Canadian Rockies."

Gail's face wrinkled in confusion. "The Canadian Rockies! Why, that sounds like. . ." Her face contorted into an angry scowl. "No, you couldn't have. Don't tell me you booked us on some vacation in the mountains."

"It sounds real nice."

"I don't care if it sounds nice! I'm not going to any mountain location, no way. Those places are full of bugs and animals. I'll bet the place you've got us staying at is no better than a flea bag."

"Gail, honestly, this is a top-notch hotel with all the extras. Believe me, it's the last place those two guys would think to look for us."

Gail closed her eyes in an attempt to stifle the tears. "Why, Keith? Why did you have to go and ruin my dreams again?"

"Gail, please. I had to do this."

"I know. Just like we had to elope, and we had to ride with those two weird men in the middle of the night. Now we have to change our honeymoon plans. I'm so tired of it all. If I had known you would be someone who doesn't care about my feelings, I wouldn't have married you." She turned in her seat, crossed her arms, and stared out the window.

"Gail, please," he begged again. "This will give us time to be by ourselves, without someone watching our every move."

"Can't you call your father and tell him not to send these men of his to Paris? I mean, this is supposed to be our honeymoon, after all. We certainly don't need any bodyguards!"

"Pop does whatever he wants, Gail. I've never been able to change his mind."

"Humph," she snorted bitterly. "Looks to me like you're attached to him by a chain."

Keith winced as the truthful words reverberated in his ears.

There could never be a more accurate depiction of what plagued his life at that moment—a long chain that bound him to the will of his father. "You're right. Pop does run my life more than he should. That's why I'm taking these steps to break free of him. He still believes he has to run my life. Maybe the death of my older brother has something to do with it. I'm trying to break free, Gail. Eloping was one giant step in my effort to break the chain. This trip is another."

Gail inhaled a sharp breath, her gaze fixed on the brick apartment buildings comprising the borough of Yonkers in New York City. A train clacked along the tracks paralleling the freeway in apparent competition with them as the car and train strove to reach their respective destinations first. Keith and Gail were similar in that respect—each endeavored to fulfill his or her own needs as they traveled the path of life. Gail speculated to herself about Keith's motive for the change. She knew from the start he was not thrilled with a trip to Europe. At one time he had suggested they have their honeymoon in the Caribbean. Now their destination seemed as far from that as the North Pole. Did he really change their plans because of the bodyguards or was there some other, unspoken reason?

"Well, I guess I don't have much choice in the matter," she mumbled. "I only wish I could do something for a change."

"When we get there, Gail, you can do whatever you want."

She raised an eyebrow. "Really?"

Keith crossed his chest with two fingers. "I promise. Whatever you want. If you want to spend each day lounging in the hot tub with room service all week, or you want to buy out the mall in Calgary, it's your choice."

Gail relaxed as these pleasant images drifted in her mind. Keith did have a wealthy family, after all. She decided that if she couldn't go to Europe, she would at least spend a huge wad of money as payback for the sheer lunacy of being forced to endure a honeymoon in the mountains of Canada.

⋰

Gail snuggled next to Keith, her head resting on his shoulder, while he read an airline magazine as they flew toward their Canadian destination. So far, he could not have been more pleased with how things were going. Upon their arrival at Kennedy Airport, Gail and he spent most of their time waiting around at the car rental agency until the last moment before their flight was scheduled to leave. Once the time drew near, they appeared like a confused young couple, dashing through check-in, then airline inspections. They reached the departure gate just as the attendant was set to lock the door leading to the aircraft.

"You just made it," she told them with a smile.

Keith had been so busy as he waded through the crowd in search of their gate, that he did not even have time to find out if Grant was following him. Now that they were safely in flight at thirty thousand feet, he spent a few minutes walking up and down the aisle, examining the passengers. To his relief, he found no one resembling the two men sent by his father. Keith returned to his leather seat in first class, silently proclaiming victory over his opponent.

"At least this flight is better," Gail commented, snuggling up to his arm. "I usually get so airsick."

"Is that why you have the motion sickness bag on your lap?" Keith asked with a grin.

"That's why. But I don't think I'll need it. We can use it as a doggie bag for all that great airline food."

Keith rolled his eyes. "Don't say anything more or I may have to borrow the bag."

Gail smiled. A flight attendant strolled by and asked how they were this evening.

"Just fine," Keith told her with confidence.

"We're on our honeymoon," Gail added.

"Congratulations! When was the wedding?"

"Well, uh. . . ," Gail faltered, giving Keith a sideways glance.

"We decided we couldn't wait and eloped," he told her. "When we get back from our honeymoon, we'll throw a big party and invite all the relatives."

The attendant nodded. "A friend of mine did the same thing. Of course the parents weren't too happy about it, but once they had the party, everyone was fine."

"That's what we're hoping," Keith said before returning his attention to the magazine.

After a few minutes, they were surprised to see the flight attendant return with a huge bottle of champagne, decorated with a bright red ribbon. "This is from the airline with our compliments," she said, proceeding to uncork the bottle.

Gail giggled as she watched the champagne sparkle in the crystal goblets set before them. Keith held up his glass to proclaim a toast. "To the most wonderful woman in the world—and the only one who could put up with all these arrangements and not lose her cool completely."

Gail smiled and sipped the champagne before placing the goblet on the table. "I really shouldn't drink much of this," she confessed. "I can get tipsy pretty fast. Dorrie says I shouldn't drink at all."

"Is that another one of your sister's no-no's from the Christian rule book?" he scoffed.

"Well, she believes drinking causes more harm than good. I've had major problems whenever I drink, so she may be right."

"That's why I never bother associating with Christians. They follow too many rules. There's no freedom at all. Besides, the Bible can be interpreted in so many ways. Who knows what's really right and what's wrong?"

"All I can say is, both Dorrie and Mick are pretty committed to what's written in there. And Mick's mother, who also is a Christian, believes like they do. Dorrie says God can show you what the Bible means. She says you can't go by man's interpretation."

Keith opened up the magazine. "I find it way too constricting. Rules, regulations, laws—who needs them?"

Gail stared at him in puzzlement. "But every society needs laws, Keith. Without them, people would be killing and stealing from one another."

Keith flipped a page. "They do that anyway, even with all the laws on the books. If you ask me, I think men make laws just so people can break them and get away with it."

"Well, I'm thankful that we have a judicial system that tries to defend the rights of victims while punishing criminals. I mean, look at Mick's father. Do you think it's right for the person who shot him to walk away without paying for his crime? I mean, Mick's dad was just handing out pamphlets in the street."

"Let me tell you, that preacher was doing a lot more than just handing out pamphlets."

"Huh?"

Keith flushed, realizing his blunder. "What I meant is, he must've done something more than hand out brochures to get that gang all riled up. I think he should've stayed off the street and in his church where he belonged. Then he wouldn't have gotten hurt, right?"

Gail sat in silence, unsure of what she believed.

"Weren't you telling me you're worried about your brother-in-law because he's following in the same footsteps as his father? In fact, even your sister is concerned that something might happen to him. Why take the risk? Be safe and stay off the street."

"Dorrie did mention her fears to me. But she's willing to trust God with Mick's life. I don't understand how she can have that kind of trust. It makes me wonder how someone can believe God for life and death situations. Mick feels the same way. He believes that sharing the Bible is worth the risk."

"Those beliefs seem to make people do crazy things, if you ask me. That's what they all are—crazy."

Gail fell silent under his cynicism. Her discomfort persisted even as the plane began its descent into the city of Calgary, Alberta. Keith bubbled over with descriptions of the various trips he had made in his lifetime. Gail listened thoughtfully, all the while questioning the internal makeup of the man sitting beside her. There was something disturbing about him, yet she could not put her finger on what it was.

As the plane touched down, Keith gripped her hand in his, whispering, "We're going to have a great time."

Gail only shrugged. Her moodiness continued as they retrieved their luggage from baggage claim, then proceeded through customs. Only when they stood waiting for a bus to take them to the car rental agency did Keith mention her melancholy.

"You're still mad that we didn't go to Paris, aren't you? Look, I promise I'll make it up to you. Just give me a chance, okay? Please don't turn to stone on me, or neither one of us will have a good time."

Inside the rental car, heading toward the resort high in the mountains, Keith's patience finally ran out. "You're driving me up the wall with this silent routine," he complained. "Is this how you're going to act the entire trip?"

Gail bit her lip and continued to stare out the window.

"Please answer my question!" he shouted.

The tone of his voice sent her head spinning and tears erupted in her eyes.

Keith drove the car off the highway and into an abandoned gravel lot. "All right, we're going to sit here until you tell me what this is all about. I don't care if we're here all night, but I deserve to know why you're acting this way."

Gail remained silent.

His fist banged the steering wheel. "All right, maybe I should have let you traipse off to your beloved Paris. Then you would have witnessed firsthand what I protected you from. You think I'm only looking out for number one. Well, you're dead wrong, Gail. I happen to love you enough to keep you away from two hoodlums who would like nothing better than to use you against me." He thrust his head back against the seat. "The problem is, they aren't here and you're *still* fighting against me."

"Why would those two men use me against you?" Her voice quivered.

Keith opened his mouth to rattle off an answer, but instead he paused and said, "I'd rather not go into that."

"Well then, now you know why I'm silent. You're like a mystery. During the flight here and at the airport, I've been trying to figure you out. I don't know what makes you tick anymore. I used to think I knew, but ever since I came back from Boston, things have been different between us. When I saw you give the customs officer that birth certificate, it suddenly dawned on me that you're hiding things from me. For instance, your last name isn't Hampton, is it?"

His face flushed. Fingers slowly tightened around the steering wheel. "Are you kidding? Of course it is."

"No, it's Costello, right?"

"Where did you come up with that?"

"Keith, I saw the painting of your family hanging in the sitting room the night we visited your parents' estate. I saw the parents, the two boys, and the name Costello engraved on a plate beneath the portrait. I knew when I met your father that he was the man in the painting, but it didn't occur to me until now that you were one of the boys. Why did you change your name?"

Keith licked his parched lips while sifting his brain for a response. He thought of concocting some story about a long-lost cousin, but feared it would backfire like everything else. "Okay, you're right. My last name is Costello. And you might as well know that my first name is not Keith, either."

"What is it?"

"Quintin."

"Quintin?" She pondered this for a moment until she remembered watching him fish out the certificate bearing the name Quintin Costello and hand it to the customs official. "Of course, the name on the birth certificate!"

"My friends used to call me Quin. Quintin sounds like an executive, or some congressman."

"Quin. I like that. It fits you better. But why did you change your name to Keith Hampton?"

He exhaled a loud sigh. "Look, can't we drive on to the resort? It's getting late and the rental agency says the hotel's a two-hour drive from Calgary. We'll discuss this some other time."

Gail stole a glance out the window as they proceeded down the highway. Despite the late hour, the sky remained bright with the final rays of the setting sun, offering views of the snowcapped mountain range. Above them loomed a bank of rocky cliffs that stood like a silent sentinel, frosted with snow. "This is a pretty area," she confessed. "It looks like Switzerland."

"Yeah, it does."

"So why did you change your name?"

"You aren't gonna let that drop, are you?" he shot back.

"Let's just say the name came with a lot of memories I wanted to leave behind. I thought that by changing my name and getting a different job, I might free myself up a little. You know how you told me that I'm too dependent on my father? Well, the name change was my declaration of independence—my rebellion against the family hierarchy, I guess you could say."

"I've heard of people changing their names," Gail remarked. "I just wish you had told me about it earlier. It makes me wonder what else you're hiding."

Quin sighed. "Remember the game of Stratego? How a player reveals his pieces as the game is played?"

"I know, but—"

"Well, I'll reveal things about myself step by step. For now let's just concentrate on having a good time on our honeymoon and forget about our families, names, and everything else."

"Shall I call you Quin instead of Keith? I mean, that is your real name."

"You can call me whatever you want, so long as we can enjoy our honeymoon. Agreed?"

Gail nodded, allowing his hand to slip over hers and give a tight squeeze. Yet, she could not settle the disturbing feeling that there was much more to the man than what she knew. While Gail had never been one to analyze others as her sister did, she could not help but be drawn to the mystery that enshrouded her husband. She decided she must find out everything there was to know about the man named Quintin Costello.

nine

When they arrived at the Chateau Lake Louise, Gail exhaled a sigh that mirrored her awe. In the atrium of the hotel, built at the turn of the century, they saw paneled walls, thick carpets, and a spiral staircase leading to a dining room and indoor pool. On a brochure, they read that the grand hotel had begun as a simple log chalet nestled beside an alpine lake; by 1900, it had become a full-scale hotel renamed Chateau Lake Louise. Gail stood expectantly next to Quin as he confirmed their reservations at the desk. Given the late hour of their arrival, the lobby was empty of the stream of tourists that typically would be seen at the hotel bordering the pristine lake. They followed a bellboy and a rolling cart containing their luggage to the top floor. The young man unlocked the door to reveal a beautifully appointed suite with all the amenities, including a second bottle of champagne resting in a silver bowl. Gail ventured to the balcony of the room overlooking the lake to see the hotel lights glimmering upon the placid waters. Goose bumps rose on her skin as the chilly mountain air shocked her flesh.

"It's cold here," she remarked, rubbing her arms to generate some warmth. "I didn't pack the proper clothing for a place like this."

"We'll go shopping," Quin promised. "The receptionist told me about the shops in Banff, which is about an hour's drive from here. I'll buy you a whole new wardrobe."

Gail unzipped one of her suitcases and donned a sweater before returning to the balcony. She settled into a chair to gaze into the night. Quin soon joined her, two glasses of champagne in his hand.

"Let's drink to our honeymoon," he said, handing her a glass.

Gail clinked his glass and took a tiny sip before placing it on the stone flooring beneath her seat. She cupped her chin in her hand, suddenly apprehensive at the idea of spending a honeymoon with a man who had only just revealed his true identity minutes before they arrived here. While they were married legally by the state, she realized the marriage certificate bore the name of Keith Hampton, not Quintin Costello. He seemed like a stranger, rather than the one she loved.

Quin set down his glass, rose, and knelt beside her, gently massaging her shoulders with his fingers. Instead of the gesture relaxing her, she felt her tension increase. *How can I go through with this honeymoon? None of what I've seen these last few days reassures me that he's the man I married.* Gail shot out of the chair at that moment, upsetting the champagne glass at her feet. The smell of alcohol rose to her nostrils, prompting a wave of nausea.

"What's the matter?" he asked.

"I, uh. . . ," she began as he stood and placed his arms around her.

"Just relax," he whispered, nibbling on her earlobe. "We've waited a long time to be alone, and now we have a whole week to discover everything about each other. I can't wait."

Gail turned away from him and leaned against the railing. "I don't know who you are. I thought I married Keith Hampton. Now that I've discovered you're this Costello person, you're like a stranger to me."

He laughed. "Gail, c'mon. I'm still the friendly waiter who helped you up from the floor at your sister's wedding. I haven't changed."

Gail did not find this situation humorous. "That man was Keith. You're not. I. . .I want my old Keith back."

The comment sent a wave of distress rippling across his face. "Gail, I'm right here! I'm the same guy. Look, if it makes you feel any better, continue calling me Keith."

"It's not just the name, it's your family, the painting, the wealthy estate—all the things I never knew about you."

"Sometimes there are things you don't know about a person until after the marriage."

"Well, that's true. I knew nothing until we got married. Now it's like I've given my whole self to some stranger in the street. I don't love a stranger."

Quin threw up his hands before plunking himself down in a chair. "I don't believe this. Now that we're on our honeymoon, alone for the first time since we got married, you decide you don't love me."

Gail sniffed. "I love Keith Hampton, a waiter turned computer repairman. I didn't marry a Quintin Costello who has wealthy parents and strange men following him wherever he goes." She dried the tears on the sleeve of her sweater.

Quin rose from his seat and stroked her arm with his fingers. "Gail, I love you. Don't you think that maybe the mask I've worn is simply a way of protecting you?"

"Sometimes I think I'd rather face the danger than all this secrecy, Keith—I mean Quin." She blew out a frustrated sigh. "You see? I don't even know what to call you! This whole thing has divided us because I don't know the real you."

Quin stood still and silent as a war of conflict raged within him. He realized more than ever his selfishness in keeping Gail while trying to conceal his past. He wanted to protect her from the evil but only succeeded in raising a wall between them. Slowly, he blew out the air from his lungs, forming a cloud in the cold mountain air. "Well, since you're so unhappy about marrying an impostor, I'll give you a choice. We can stay here and try to make this work, or we can go home tomorrow and forget this ever happened. I know I've been secretive, but there are reasons for it. I've asked you time and time again to trust me. If you were to find out certain things, it could have severe repercussions." He lifted his eyes to acknowledge the star-strewn sky above them. "I thought I could keep you from all this, but I knew the night we arrived at my father's house that I would never be able to conceal my life from you. Pop tried to conceal his life from my mother, and now she's gone because of it."

"What do you mean?"

"I didn't want you to know the truth about her. I wanted you to think she's alive when she's. . ." He paused as the grief clogged his throat. In a choking voice, he said, "She's dead. She committed suicide."

Gail's mouth fell open. In an instant she was on her feet.

"It happened about three years ago. I kept her death hidden inside me, afraid to face the pain of it, just like my father."

"So there's only the two of you. . .you and your father?"

He nodded.

"Now I see why your father wants to control you." Gail shook her head as she wrapped an arm around his shoulders. "That's terrible. Why did she do it?"

"She was upset about my brother's death. Mother always loved Archie more than me. When he died in the car accident, she never got over it. There were clashes between her and my father. Pop and I left for a business trip in Europe; when we returned, she was in intensive care at the hospital after overdosing on alcohol and sedatives. I saw her once, but that was it. I never got to tell her good-bye." A tear escaped down his cheek.

"Oh, Keith, I'm so sorry," Gail murmured, hugging him close.

"I know she never loved me, but I wanted her to." His voice cracked as his wet cheeks reflected the light of the lampposts lining the walkway below. "I was mad when she died. I didn't want anyone to know. Now I miss her so much. I wish I could tell her that I understand why she was so sad. I–I wish she could be here for us."

"Oh, Keith," Gail moaned, shaking her head. "I don't know what to say."

Quin wiped the tears from his face. "There's nothing you can say."

"You've been through so much with the loss of your brother and mother. In a way, you're very much like Mick. He went through the same kind of tragedy with his father. Dorrie was able to help him when no one else could."

Quin grimaced at the mention of Mick's father and looked away.

"We really need to visit Dorrie and Mick after this trip," Gail said.

"After this trip? I thought you didn't want to stay here."

"I think we should stay and spend this time getting to know one another. We need to be honest and get our lives out in the open. If you are willing to do that, then I think everything will be better between us."

Quin shook his head. "I can't do that."

"What?"

"I can't tell you everything. Don't make me, Gail."

Her face fell. "So I have to live in a marriage full of secrets, is that it? I'm not going to do that. I won't. If we can't be honest with one another, then there's no sense in going on with this relationship." She whirled back to face the night. "I hate this place. It's so cold. It's. . .it's dark and eerie. I'm just not strong enough to deal with any of this."

Quin stood still and silent. Finally, he turned and walked back into the suite. "Fine. Then we won't go on. I've just finished telling you of some of the worst pain inside me, and you decide you still want to dump me. Super. I'll make arrangements for us to leave tomorrow." He picked up his suitcase and slammed the door as he went out.

The noise echoed in her ears. Gail threw herself down on the bed. She felt confused and lost, without a sense of direction for her life. How could everything that had seemed so right in the beginning turn out so wrong? Tears dampened her pillow. Dorrie had known there was something wrong with Keith. She had sensed it, but Gail had only pushed her warnings aside. Now she felt trapped with a man she knew nothing about, and who was unwilling to tell her anything. She continued to weep until there were no more tears left to shed.

Finally, she rose and went to the dresser. She opened a drawer; a Bible was inside. Her hand curved around the book and pulled it out. "Okay, God," she said aloud, her hand shaking. "I'm at the end of the road here. I just don't know what to do. Help me find the answers, please, before I go crazy!" She settled herself on the bed, propped up by several fluffy pillows, and began to read. Scripture after Scripture spoke of God's love for her and His desire for her to understand Him. She lifted her eyes, remembering that Dorrie had once said that to know the purposes of God, you must be willing to surrender your life to Him. "What does that mean?" she wondered, gazing about the ornate room until her eyes fell on the phone. Dorrie. Dorrie would know. Dorrie would help her understand this awful situation. Despite the late hour, she dialed her sister's number in Boston with trembling fingers.

The groggy voice of Mick answered the ring. In the background she could hear Dorrie say, "Two A.M.! If it's Corky again, you hang up, Mick. I mean it."

"Mick, it's me, Gail. Please, I need to speak to Dorrie."

"Gail?" came Dorrie's voice. "Honey, what's wrong?" Fresh tears spurted from Gail's eyes at the concern in her sister's voice.

Forty minutes later Gail was still on the phone, yet now a tremendous peace filled her heart. During the conversation, Gail had acknowledged the emptiness in her life. With Dorrie's help, Gail reached out to the living God and found Him willing to fill the emptiness, to accept her into His family. Now she felt a peace greater than anything she had ever known. With God in her heart, she was able to confess to Dorrie everything she had learned about Quin and his family.

"I don't love him anymore," Gail said. "He lied to me about everything."

"Oh, Gail," came the voice that soothed like balm pouring over her wounded soul. "I know this is hard, but you must think of Quin as someone who needs God. He doesn't understand what he's doing. Before you do anything else, read 1 Corinthians 13. It's the chapter about love. Although you don't feel like you love him right now, because of what he's done, read for yourself what God says about love."

"He isn't the man I fell in love with. He's an impostor." She began to cry. "I gave my innocence away to an imposter. . .to a man I don't even know anymore! I can't be married to someone like him."

"You need to find out who you did marry, Gail. You can't go back on the vows you said to him, even if he used a different name. The vows we make are for life. Let God help you love Quin and understand him. Don't try to do it by yourself. You found out tonight that you can't handle it alone. Now that God is in your heart, you are never alone. He will help you. Always remember that."

"I'll try."

"Just enjoy yourself while you're there. Let go and let God, I always say. Remember how I'm trusting God for Mick. You are a babe in Christ right now, but you're going to have to grow up quickly and trust God for Quin. And when you get back home, come see us as soon as possible. I think it would do Quin good to talk to Mick. They share similar stories of pain with their family members."

"I will, Dorrie. Thanks so much."

"You've made me happy as a lark," Dorrie exclaimed. "We'll be praying for you."

"Thanks."

When Gail hung up the phone, she sensed the love of God flowing through her heart. All those questions she had about Dorrie's faith in an unseen God had been answered. After experiencing His love and forgiveness, God reigned in Gail's own life now. As she readied herself for bed, Gail decided that she must help Quin discover this personal Savior and friend himself. She would try to reach out to his heart, and in the process, find a new love for him that only God could supply.

❧

Gail slept well in the enormous bed, only to be awakened the next morning by the telephone ringing. She rose up on one elbow and reached for the receiver.

"Hello?"

"It's me."

A smile broke out on her face. "Oh, Quin, you won't believe what happened to me."

"Look, I wanted to let you know that the bellboy will be up in half an hour to collect your luggage. I booked us a flight back to New York that's leaving in four hours. That gives us two hours for the drive back to Calgary and plenty of time to go through customs before boarding."

Gail's face fell as her hands clenched the receiver. "But

Quin, I don't want to leave."

"You'll be home in no time, ready to get on with your life. . . ." He paused. "What did you say?"

"I said I don't want to leave." Her eyes glimpsed the bright sunshine streaming through the parted curtains. "It's a new day, Quin. I feel brand new on the inside, just like the gorgeous day outside."

"You seem different this morning. I thought you hated being here. I recall the words very clearly. 'Dark,' 'cold'. . ."

"Not anymore. I love it here."

"What made you change your mind?"

"God," Gail said reverently.

"God," Quin repeated before chuckling in scorn. "How did God perform that miracle? Send the archangel to your room last night?"

The comment drew Gail away from the window. "No. I was really upset about what happened between us. I read the Bible for a while after you left. Then I talked to Dorrie."

"You mean you called your sister in Boston?"

"Yes, and she told me all about getting saved."

"Getting saved, huh? Saved from what?"

"You know, from your sins and everything."

Quin sighed in exasperation. "Look, Gail, if you're going to fill my head with a lot of religious nonsense, then I'll take that next flight out of here. You know how I feel about Christianity. A lot of do-gooders bent on following a bunch of rules."

"But God is real, Quin. He spoke to me last night."

"He spoke to you." Quin snapped his fingers over the phone. "So just like that, you're now religious? Wow, and you complain that you can't figure me out! Look who's hiding things now? So how long have you really believed in this Christianity stuff—the whole time and only now you've decided to tell me?"

"I didn't believe anything until last night," Gail said earnestly. "Dorrie explained it to me. I prayed with her and—"

"And now you're instantly changed. Well, if it's all right with you, why don't we just set this God stuff aside and try to figure out what we're going to do. That is, if you care to be around me anymore."

"Of course I do. I want to stay." She padded across the floor, stretching the telephone cord to the limit so she could view the breathtaking scenery outside the balcony doors. The snowpack in the crevices of the mountains glistened in the morning sunlight. "Have you seen how beautiful it is here?"

"No, I've been in a phone booth calling for flight reservations. I didn't sleep a wink all night, either. The lobby was like a freezer. I'm stiff and my neck has a crick in it or something."

"Then come up here with me. It's nice and warm. There's even a hot tub."

"Excuse me? Am I hearing you right? Just last night you didn't care if you were even with me."

"This is the perfect place for a new beginning, Quin."

She sensed his confusion on the phone. "Well, okay. If you want to stay, I'll cancel the plane reservations."

Gail hung up the phone. She felt like soaring on one of the wispy clouds that drifted across the azure sky. She replaced the receiver, then skipped over to the doors leading to the balcony and opened them. A blast of cold air hit her face. Everything appeared new to her, fresh and alive, reflecting a beauty she had never known in her life. "Oh, thank you, Lord!" she breathed, inhaling the sweet fragrance of the tall ponderosa pine trees dotting the steep mountainsides. "Thank you, Lord, for allowing me to see Your creation with new eyes this morning. Oh, Dorrie, you are so right! You *can* see God in the mountains!"

Today was a new day, and with God's help, she would make it through.

ten

"You really are different," Quin observed as Gail brushed out her curly hair before the huge mirror. "I mean, you look the same and all, but there's something different...." He couldn't help but notice the change when he had arrived back at the room, suitcase in hand, to find the hot tub filling and Gail greeting him with open arms. He had felt it was like awakening to a new morning after a nightmare. He had pushed the change in her aside to bask in their love, but now stared at her in wonder.

"Well, I'm starving," Gail announced. "Do they serve breakfast around here?"

"They're serving a buffet breakfast right now, in the Poppy Room."

Gail threw the brush on the counter. "Great. Let's go. Then maybe we can decide on what to do."

"I figured you'd probably want to go shopping or just lounge around," Quin remarked as they headed for the elevator.

"Are you kidding? I'm not going to waste this gorgeous day. It's too pretty to spend it in a store."

Quin eyed her in puzzlement. Could this be the same woman he married? Gail seemed like a stranger; it was as if she existed on some other level than he did. Now he understood all too well Gail's distress concerning his identity. Inside the spacious dining room, he could not even look out the huge plate glass window that revealed the blue waters of the alpine lake, framed by the rugged mountains.

"Oh, look at that, Quin!" Gail breathed as she raced over

to peer out the window. "Have you ever seen anything so beautiful in all your life?"

"I don't know," he said glumly as they took their seats. After serving themselves from the buffet, he focused his attention on his plate of food. His fork stabbed at the fruit chunks while Gail stared out the window. Finally, he threw down his fork and said in all earnestness, "Look, Gail, you don't need to do this for me."

"Do what?"

"Pretend you like this place. I know you don't. You made it clear to me that you would rather be in Europe. There's no sense in hiding the fact behind this facade of yours."

"I'm not hiding anything," she said cheerfully. "I'm just seeing how pretty everything is. It's like I woke up to a whole new world."

"Believe me, it's the same cruddy ol' world out there," he said flatly, stirring cream into his coffee.

"Not when God's in it."

Quin leaned back in his chair and crossed his arms. "Look, Gail, I don't know what's come over you, but I'm begging you to put an end to this. I'm really sorry I didn't tell you who I was from the beginning. Please don't play the same game with me."

She reached out her hand to him. "Quin, I'm not playing a game. This is for real. God came into my heart last night. It's like what we talked about before we left on this trip—about being born again and starting over. I know what that means now. Everything is different. It's like the old me passed away and a new Gail has taken her place."

"Please, I want the old Gail back, even if we weren't getting along."

Gail shook her head as she resumed drinking her coffee. "I don't want that person back again. Never in a million years."

Quin fell silent. Perhaps he deserved this. After all, hadn't he been playing a similar game with Gail? Only now it was his turn to be the victim and he didn't like it one bit.

After breakfast, Gail bustled over to the activity desk with Quin trailing far behind. She engaged the receptionist in lively chatter about things to see and do in the area. With a pile of literature in her hand, she found a padded arm chair and sat down to sift through all their options. "Listen to this, Quin. You can take horses up to a neat rock formation just behind the chalet. There's an English teahouse up there and everything."

"That's nice," he said, playing with the button on his rugby shirt.

"And look at this." She held up a pamphlet outlining a gondola ride to the summit of a great mountain. "Doesn't the view look beautiful? Let's do that, too."

Quin said nothing. He continued to play with the button until it popped off the shirt. Gail looked over to see the button resting in his hand. "Oh, Quin. Maybe we can find someone to fix it."

"Who cares? I just want someone to fix us."

Gail appeared to ignore his comment and motioned to him with her hand. "C'mon, I want to put on jeans before we go horseback riding."

"I can't even imagine you on a horse," he scoffed.

"I can't, either, but that's what makes this so fun! I feel like I can try new things." She paused to consider the statement. "Maybe that's why Mick can do his work without fear. God gives him the strength. We all have fear. It's ingrained in us. But that fear just goes away when God is there."

Quin wondered about her statement as they headed back to their suite. He had never allowed fear to establish a foothold in his life, but now he suddenly felt afraid. He was afraid of

Gail and what she had become. Still, if she had not changed, there would be no marriage or honeymoon. Thinking of the special time they had shared that morning, was it really so awful that Gail had found peace with God? She had poured out her love to him, and now she was delighted with the destination he had selected for their honeymoon. The consequences appeared positive, but the change in her made him feel unworthy. Perhaps that is why he wanted the old Gail back, whether the marriage suffered or not. He could not face the sin that stained his soul.

⁊ა

Despite his discomfort, Quin enjoyed himself on the excursion into the pristine mountains. The weather was picture perfect as they rode on horseback to a rock formation known as the Bee Hives, perched high atop a cliff above the chateau. There they sampled English hospitality at a quaint log teahouse. Gail seemed more beautiful than ever to Quin, with her radiant smile and shining eyes. After the meal, he sneaked her into the woods behind the teahouse and gave her a kiss.

"You are so lovely," he told her, pushing back her curly hair with his fingers and gazing into her face. "Even if you do get into this God of yours and all, I still love you."

"And I love you."

He raised an eyebrow. "Do you really?"

Gail nodded. "Really. I'm still learning how to do it, of course. It takes time."

They walked hand and hand to the hitching post where the horses were tethered. "I'm amazed how quickly you picked up horseback riding," he commented.

"It was a little scary," she admitted, "but I just kept concentrating on other things, like the woods, or the scenery. In no time I was really enjoying the ride. Maybe we can own horses someday."

Quin chuckled and helped her up onto the animal. "That's a new one. My little Gail, owning a horse farm."

"It seems unreal, I know. But 'I can do all things through Christ who strengthens me.' I read that verse this morning while you were in the shower."

Quin fell silent as they followed their guide back down the trail. He watched Gail sway to and fro on the horse, her hair flying in the breeze, her face acknowledging her surroundings with a joy he could not understand. *Help me understand what's going on with her,* he found himself thinking. Quin paused when he caught himself praying for the first time in his life. *She's affecting me more than I realize.*

❧

The next day, they drove in the sporty rental car to the quaint village of Banff, where Quin bought Gail an assortment of fashions at the little shops dotting the streets. They ate lunch at the famous Banff Springs Hotel, which appeared like a great castle in the midst of a pine forest. Afterward, they strolled along the green of the famous golf course surrounding the hotel, where numerous elk feasted on the succulent grass. Quin tried to think of things to say, but his mind was blank. He found nothing worthy of her interest. Gail, on the other hand, filled his ears with stories of her youth, her days as a cheerleader in high school, and the excursion she took with Dorrie in the mountains.

They paused at a wooden bridge spanning a creek. "I found out during our trip to the White Mountains how different Dorrie and I were," Gail said. "Sometimes I really hated her Christianity. She seemed to know everything, and I felt like a dust speck without a brain. But during these last few weeks, I've come to understand that she really does care about me." Gail glanced up to find Quin staring off into space. "It means something when someone cares for you."

"Yeah, it does."

"I know you mentioned believing your mother didn't care for you."

"No, she didn't."

"But you got along with your father?"

Quin snorted. "Sure, as long as I did whatever he wanted. I thought it was real cool, you know, getting involved with his precious work. Pop prides himself on one thing—his business. He's greedy and he's selfish. I suppose that's where I picked up those traits. He wants things done his way, and he makes his fortune the only way he knows how. I'm trying to get myself out from under it all. That's why I went to such pains to change my name, and wear eyeglasses, and take mundane jobs like a waiter or some kind of computer wizard. I wanted to get out of the whole mess."

Gail narrowed her eyebrows questioningly. "What exactly does your father do?"

Quin picked up a small oval stone and pitched it into the creek. "It's kind of complicated. He's into sales, I guess you could say."

"What does he sell?"

"Expensive merchandise. He gets a hold of it at a cheap price, then sells it off to the highest bidder. He comes away rolling in cash, but that's about it."

"I guess you learned that money isn't everything."

"It's nothing. It buys trips, clothes, even wedding rings. But it doesn't buy love." He turned to Gail. "I can tell it didn't buy your love. At first you seemed to like the presents and the idea of marrying into wealth. But a few nights ago, when you found out I wasn't Keith Hampton, you were willing to throw it all away. What made you change your mind to stick it out with me?"

"Well, Dorrie helped me. She said I made a vow to you,

even if it was before the justice of the peace and with a different identity. I made a vow to stay married to you as a person, no matter what. She said I couldn't walk away from something like that. And she told me to read 1 Corinthians 13. It's a chapter all about love. It says that love bears all things and it lasts." Gail brought forth her hand, glittering with the large diamonds embedded in both rings. "I know these rings won't last, even though they are beautiful. But the love behind the gift of these rings will. That's all that matters anyway."

"Can love heal the past too?" he asked softly. "Can it forgive?"

Gail looked into his face to see the pain in his eyes. "Yes," she told him, cupping his cheeks in her hands. "It can." She reached out to kiss him.

Quin was moved by her touch that eased his aching heart. For the first time he felt an internal joy. Perhaps a little of the joy that bubbled up within Gail had rubbed off on him. He found the sensation a welcome relief, after all he had endured.

&

Gail ran the water in the shower stall of their suite until it was piping hot. She hoped the steam might warm her chilled limbs after a drenching rain had caught her and Quin off guard while they headed back to the car at the Banff Springs golf course. A shower would also refresh her for the evening's activities. Quin had urged her to dress up tonight, for they were going to the best restaurant at the hotel. She felt invigorated by the warm spray that streamed over her face. The day had gone well, despite her apprehension. Quin responded eagerly to the love that Gail ministered with God's help, much like a withering plant in need of moisture. Gail thought about the similarity while the water coursed down her face. Quin's sad features and the stories of his past conjured up the image of a plant dying in a drought. As the water ran through her fingers, she thought of love flowing like the water, reaching into his heart, refreshing him and restoring him to life.

She stepped out of the stall and dried off quickly, then spent time applying her makeup. She took extra care to appear nice for Quin in the hope that it might speak to his heart and strengthen their relationship. After dressing in an ankle-length gown, she sat in a chair and waited for him to return from running a few errands. During her wait, she watched the sun sink behind the glacier. The remaining sunlight cast an orange hue across Lake Louise and the surrounding mountain peaks. A few courageous people were still seen paddling canoes across the chilly water while enjoying the sunset.

After what seemed like an eternity, Quin finally arrived. When she opened the door, the odor of alcohol wafted into the room.

"You were drinking?" Gail asked.

"I had a few drinks before I came back here. Is that a problem?"

"Well, I don't know." Gail tried to mask her disappointment by slipping a hand under his arm. After the encouraging signs during their walk at Banff Springs, she had hoped there might be changes stirring within him.

"By the way, you look ravishing in black."

"Thanks."

Quin glanced at her curiously. "There's something wrong, isn't there?"

Gail pretended to fiddle with the gold clasp of her black clutch purse. "Well, you told me you were going to run a few errands. I didn't know that meant having drinks at the bar."

Quin paused in the hallway before the bank of elevators. His dark eyebrows narrowed. "So now that you're a Christian, that means I have to stop having fun?"

"No, I didn't say that."

"But you're implying it."

"Well, maybe I don't want to see you hurt. You see, I was hurt by alcohol once. I. . ." Gail paused. "I was nearly raped while I was drunk one night. It was terrible. I will never forget it. I learned that drinking only hurts people, Quin. It makes you lose your senses. You do things you wouldn't normally do. It messes up your mind, and I don't want your mind messed up. I love your mind just the way it is."

He cracked a small grin. "Well, thanks. Okay, I won't drink. I didn't know it would upset you so much."

Gail snuggled against his arm, inhaling the spicy scent of his aftershave.

"And don't worry; I didn't just leave to get drunk," he assured her as they walked into an elevator. "I ran my errands."

They arrived in the Edelweiss dining room, where a waiter led them to a small table beside a plate-glass window overlooking the lake. A candle decorated the table, and next to the candle was a huge vase of red roses.

"Oh, they're beautiful, Quin!" Gail gushed. When she took her place across from him, she noticed a small package, wrapped in a gold bow, sitting on her dinner plate. "What's this?"

"A wedding gift," he told her. "You gave me yours, so here's mine."

She blushed as she tore the wrapper off and opened a case. Inside was a simple gold locket in the shape of a heart. "Why, it's beautiful!"

"Simple," he told her with a wink. "Not extravagant, not flashy. Just plain simple."

"I love it. Please put it on me." Gail moved to his side of the table and sat on his lap while Quin opened the clasp. As he positioned the necklace around her curved neck, he noticed a brawny man, dressed in a leather jacket, sitting alone at a table near theirs. The man appeared to be studying the menu, but every so often his dark eyes would regard Gail and Quin from above the menu he held. Quin gave Gail a swift kiss on her cheek before ushering her back to her seat. Once or twice he turned his head to watch the man at the table nearby. Quin did not recognize him from any past contact. He tried to remove the stranger from his thoughts and concentrate on ordering dinner.

"So what's on the docket for tomorrow?" Quin inquired as he tackled the appetizer brought to him—smoked salmon on a bed of crisp greens.

"I don't really know. I haven't thought that far."

"Maybe we can take a nice long drive," he remarked. "Maybe up the Icefields Parkway to Jasper National Park."

Gail's eyes brightened. "I was reading up a little on it. There's a glacier you can walk on, or you can take a tour in one of those big snow coaches."

"Fine. We'll do that. As I said at the beginning of our honeymoon, whatever Gail wants, Gail gets."

She frowned and laid down her fork. "Quin, you make me sound really selfish. Why don't we do something you want?"

"I am. I'm with you."

"No, really. What would you like to do?"

Quin thought about it, and when he did, he sensed the man staring at them from across the way. A strange feeling, like sharp prickles, ran up and down his back. It was the feeling of being watched. "We'll talk about it later," he said in a whisper.

Their dinners arrived, tastefully garnished with edible flowers and fruit. Gail slowly ate hers, relishing every delicious bite. After a time, she glanced up to see that he had not eaten one bite.

"Why aren't you eating, Quin? Is something wrong?"

He shook his head.

"You really should eat. The food is delicious."

He finally picked up his knife and fork and began cutting up a slice of beef, but he found his appetite had vanished. *Grant*, he thought, watching the man out of the corner of his eye. *Grant finally found out where we went and sent his goon to follow us. Oh, God, what am I going to do?*

Quin jumped from his seat in a start, pulled out a pile of bills to pay for the dinner, and took Gail by the arm. "C'mon, let's go."

"Quin, what is it? Are you sick?"

He said nothing as he walked swiftly from the dining hall and to the back stairs. "Let's. . .uh, let's go to some of those boutiques on the lower level, shall we?"

"Well, if you want. I just don't know why. . ." She paused when they came to a children's boutique. "Oh, look at the cute bears. Some are dressed as Royal Canadian Mounted Police. And look—here's one dressed in red, white, and blue, holding a little American flag in his paw. Aren't they adorable? I'm going to get both for Jamie—one from our trip and one to celebrate July Fourth next month."

Quin remained outside the shop, peering up and down the corridor while Gail bought gifts for baby Jamie—a T-shirt adorned with bighorn sheep as well as the small stuffed bears. At another shop, Gail purchased shirts with designs of mountains stitched on them for Mick and Dorrie, along with several gifts for her parents.

"Do you want to buy your father anything?" Gail asked Quin.

"No. Nothing for Pop. He doesn't need anything, at least anything worth his while."

"I remember seeing all those artifacts in the sitting room. I wonder if maybe he would like something from here for his collection?"

Quin cast her a look. "You don't want to supply that shelf, Gail."

"I guess I shouldn't ask you why."

"Right. Don't ask why."

Silent and confused, Gail trailed along as Quin led her back to the honeymoon suite. Once inside, he triple locked the doors and went out to examine the balcony.

"Quin, what's going on? You're acting really strange."

"Don't worry about it, Gail," he mumbled.

She tossed the purchases into a chair. "Please don't say that. It's the same thing you told me the night those men came to our room at the bed and breakfast. I *am* worried. You haven't been right since dinner."

He stared over the balcony at several people walking along the pathway below. Some paused to gaze out over the lake adorned with shafts of moonlight shimmering on its placid surface. Others pointed up at the hotel. Quin sucked in his breath, wondering which one of them might be his adversary. He turned to find Gail hovering at his elbow, her brown eyes wide with concern.

"Gail, listen to me. I don't want you going anywhere without me."

"Is there a problem with those men again?"

"There may be. I caught some strange-looking character staring at us at dinner tonight. He didn't look familiar to me, but I'm not going to take any chances. Grant has all kinds of low-lifes working for him. That guy may one of them."

"You think it may be one of your father's bodyguards?"

"Possibly. By now Grant knows we didn't go to Paris. He's had plenty of time to make an about-face and fly in someone to keep an eye on us."

"What are we going to do?"

Quin ran his fingers through his hair. "I'm not sure. But

you're to stay with me at all times. If things gets rough, we may have to make a fast exit out of here."

Gail threw herself into his arms. "I. . .I don't want anything to happen. Please, Quin, I'm so scared."

"Hey, it will be all right. Remember all that stuff you told me a few days ago on our horseback trip? About the fearless woman ready to tackle the world?"

Gail brushed a tear from her cheek. "Horses are one thing, strange men hiding in corners are something else. I just don't understand why your father is doing this."

Quin sighed. "Because he doesn't want me to leave."

"Huh?"

"He doesn't want me to leave the business. I'm his heir, or so he says. He wants me to pick up the reins once he leaves this world. I've refused him, and now he's getting desperate. He's putting pressure on me."

"I wish he would leave us alone."

"I wish he would, too."

eleven

"I don't think you should go," Gail said in a low voice.

"I need to. I have to."

"Can't you just ignore it?"

Quin shook his head as he ran a comb through his hair. "If I ignore this, Gail, I'll never be rid of him. At least the guy's come out of hiding. Now I can confront him and maybe get him on the next plane so we can continue with our honeymoon." He threw the comb on the table and ventured over to give her a hug. "Don't answer the door for anyone, and don't go out on the balcony, either."

"I wish you wouldn't do this," she whispered. "Please."

"It will be all right." He then added as an afterthought, "I guess you could pray for me."

"I will. I'll pray ever minute you're away."

Quin smiled. "An old heathen like me could use prayer, I'm sure." He left the room, his mind buzzing with the memory of the call from the hotel lobby, in which he was instructed to meet with someone named Andre. Quin could not recall anyone in the business with the name of Andre. When he questioned the man's identity on the phone, the voice gave specific details concerning their dinner the evening before, complete with the roses and the heart necklace. Quin's face colored when he realized his life was an open book to all the spies in the business. *I have to put a stop to this.* He pushed the button for the elevator. *If I don't, Gail and I will find ourselves hounded everywhere we go.*

Quin walked over to some chairs in front of large plate-glass windows, where he found a man dressed in a leather jacket and smoking a cigarette. He pushed down a shiver of anxiety that swept through him and took a seat. "Andre, I presume?"

"I work for Grant," he said in a foreign accent.

"So I figured. What's this all about? I don't appreciate spectators on my honeymoon."

"I have news from Grant today." He flicked ash from the cigarette into a glass tray.

"What news?"

"He say the boss-man is gone."

Quin blinked. "What?"

"He say the boss-man is gone. Dead. Grant is now the new boss."

"You're lying."

"No. I come here at first to watch you and your wife." Andre's eyes scanned the hotel. "Very nice place you pick. Then Grant calls today to tell me the boss is gone and he is the new boss. So Grant say he has no need of you. You are no longer in the business."

"I. . .I don't believe it." *Pop is dead? How could that be?* "Let me call Grant. I want to speak to him. What's his phone number?"

Andre shook his head. "Can't do it."

"Then I'm calling home." Quin jumped to his feet, only to find the hand of Andre on his arm, pulling him back down into the chair. "Don't do it, young Costello," his voice warned. "Best to leave it alone. You wanted out of the business, now you are out. Grant says to stay away."

Quin shook off the hand. "I won't have Grant or you telling me what to do. This is my father we're speaking of, and I'm his son. I deserve to know what's going on, even if you don't have any sense in you to understand the relationship between a father and son. So back off." He strode away, his mind a whirl of emotions. He went straight to the suite, where an anxious Gail paced the carpeted floor, her lips moving in prayer. She stopped short when he entered.

"Quin, what happened?"

He ignored her question and headed for the phone to dial the number of the estate. To his relief, the trusted butler named Charles answered.

"Oh, Master Costello, I'm so glad you called!"

"Charles, is it true? Is my father dead?"

"No, but he is very ill. He has been calling for you."

Quin closed his eyes as his hand gripped the phone. *That slimy snake,* he thought, remembering what Grant told Andre. *He tried to tell me my father was dead!*

"You must come right away. We think he has suffered a heart attack, but he won't go to the hospital. He only wants to see you."

"Tell Pop I'm coming home," Quin said and hung up the phone.

Gail was right behind him, listening to the conversation. "Quin, please tell me what happened. Is it your father?"

"Charles says that Pop has suffered a heart attack. I have to leave for home right away. But I want you to stay here. My father's house is no place for you right now. It's way too dangerous."

"I don't care. I'm going with you."

"Gail, I can't risk your safety. There are men with bad blood in their veins who can't wait to grab hold of the business. You could get hurt. Please stay."

"Quin, all that matters to me is you. I told you once before that I would face the danger just to know who you are. Please let me come with you. I love you."

Quin sighed. "Gail, you can't come. Look, if you don't want to stay here alone, then I'll buy you a plane ticket to your sister's place. Go see your sister in Boston and I'll join you as soon as I get through with this mess. But you must do what I say, if you love me at all."

Gail hesitated. "Well, all right. Promise me you'll come the minute everything is all right at home."

"I promise. Right now I have to get on the horn and make arrangements for the earliest flights possible for the two of us. We'll drive to Calgary tonight, find a hotel room, then catch the first plane home tomorrow. The sooner we get out of here, the better. In the meantime, you'd better let your sister know what's going on."

As his mind churned with these plans, he thought of the man named Andre and how he had tried to stop him from making the call to his father's estate. There was no telling what the man might do if he got wind of his plan to leave for home. *God, please,* he prayed, *please keep that man off our back.*

❧

Andre promptly followed Quin onto the flight to New York, obtaining a first-class seat across the aisle from him. Quin pretended to immerse himself in magazines, anything to keep his mind off the dark eyes glaring at him from across the aisle. The words on the page became a blur. Not only must he deal with his father's illness, but also the corrupt men eager to take over the business, should anything happen. Quin glanced over at Andre, wondering how loyal he was to Grant. Perhaps the man was new at the game. Quin stuffed the magazine into the pouch before him. *There's only one way to find out.*

After a few minutes, he watched the passenger next to Andre slip out of his seat to stretch his legs. Heaving a sigh, Quin took advantage of the empty seat and sat down next to the brawny man, still dressed in his leather jacket. The man stared at him in surprise.

"We meet again, Andre."

"You should not go home, young Costello."

"What? I'm not supposed to go home and pay my last respects to my father?"

"That's not what I mean."

Quin caught the hesitancy in the man's voice. "Didn't you have a father, Andre?"

"Yes, but he died when I was a boy."

"You miss him?"

A muscle twitched in the man's ebony-colored cheek.

"I'll bet you paid your last respects, didn't you? You told him how much you loved him, that sort of thing. And he told you how proud he was, and to remember that you'll always be his son."

Andre turned toward the window and said nothing. Quin could see he had struck a chord in the man.

"So how did he die?"

Andre shifted in his seat. "You ask too many questions, Costello."

"And you shouldn't be involved in any of this, Andre. I can already see that you're a decent fellow, caught up with a bunch of thugs. Hanging around Grant is not good for your health. You know that."

"Grant chose me."

"Yeah. He chooses lots of men, and then they end up on the shallow end of the stick. But stick with me in this game and I'll treat you right."

Andre lifted his eyebrows. "You mean join you?"

"Sure. Grant doesn't know half the details of running the business that I know. Stick with me and you'll be a winner. Isn't that what you want? To be a winner in life? Grant doesn't know anything about winning. He's a follower, a bellboy, a common stooge. He only does what my father tells him to do.

He isn't a leader. But Pop, the boss-man, made me a leader. I'm his son, after all. He taught me everything." Quin watched the taut lines on the man's face relax, yet the coal black eyes remained wide with interest.

"Stick with you," he repeated.

"Don't stick with losers like Grant. By the way, has he even paid you yet for your work?"

Andre shook his head.

"Well, I pay my men up front because I trust them." Quin pulled out his remaining cash from the pocket of his denim shirt. "Here. This should buy you some new clothes. Leather can smell after a while if you don't change regularly."

Andre's eyes nearly popped out of his head as he counted the cash.

"So we understand each other now?"

He nodded. "I understand. You're the boss-man's son. I understand everything."

"Fine and dandy. Now just keep this under your hat. In other words, keep quiet about this to Grant. He might throw a tantrum if he finds out you've switched sides."

Andre nodded as he stuffed the money in his pocket, just as the passenger returned from his jaunt down the aisle.

"Oh, excuse me," Quin said to the man, displaying a roguish smile as he patted Andre on the back. "An old friend of mine. He and I were just discussing how much we miss our fathers. Isn't that right, Andre?"

Andre smiled weakly. Quin returned to his seat and exhaled a sigh of relief, hoping he had just foiled Grant's ambitious plans.

Quin dreaded the meeting to come. Out of the countless conversations he'd had with his father, he knew this one would prove the most difficult. He drove straight from Albany

Airport to the family estate with Andre by his side. It amazed him how helpful the giant man had been at the airport— retrieving his luggage and arranging for a rental car. Perhaps money did talk when it came right down to it.

Inside the huge manor house of the Costello estate, all of the help gathered in the hallway in a silent vigil. Solemn expressions marked their faces. In the library sat many of the men Quin had come to know in the business—the hard faces and gnarled hands of men who had spent years in criminal activity. Quin knew that with his father's illness came the likelihood that men like Grant would jump at the chance to take control of the empire and squelch any opposition.

During the drive to the estate, Quin thought about the miraculous transformation that had occurred within Gail. He wondered about this God who changed lives, and if there was any way God might make room to help him out a little. With everything about to blow up, he desperately needed some kind of supreme being to watch over him. Prayer now stirred within his heart as he asked for guidance and wisdom.

After a few anxious minutes spent pacing in the hall, Quin saw the family physician emerge from the master suite. He led Quin into the spare bedroom that Gail had occupied the night they were brought in by Grant. Quin could tell by the expression on the physician's face that the situation was grim. "How bad is it?"

"Unless you can convince your father to go immediately to the hospital, he has no chance of recovery. His heart has been severely damaged by a blockage in one of the coronary arteries. His heartbeat is irregular and he is weakening by the hour. He needs immediate medical attention before it's too late, if it's not too late already."

"Then I'll tell him he has to go. Call the rescue squad right now."

The physician shook his head. "You know your father, Quintin. He's a stubborn man."

"Well, I can be stubborn too. We're related in that way." Quin marched out of the room and into the master bedroom where his father lay beneath the covers. He paused to watch the man's labored breathing. Perspiration trickled down the pale face as his father fought for his life. Sweat droplets on the tips of his mustache glistened like beads in the light of a lamp sitting on a night stand.

"Pop?" Quin said softly.

The patriarch turned his head and offered a faint smile. "Quintin. I knew you would come. Stand here beside me."

Quin came closer, fighting to suppress the wave of distress within him. "Pop, you've got to go to the hospital right now. I had Charles send for the rescue squad."

Anton Costello shook his head. "No. . .no, I can't."

"Pop, are you crazy? You'll die! Why are you doing this?"

"It is for the best. I make one final plea to you, Quintin. You must hear me. All my life I have trained you to take over when I am gone. I have seen this past year how you did not want anything more to do with my work. But you must reconsider." He coughed loudly, clutching his chest.

Quin stared at his father. "Pop."

"I'm dying, Quintin. Will you carry on my work or not?"

"Pop, you know I can't. You're leaving me an empire built upon greed and corruption. You have used thousands of lives for all of this." He waved his hand at the finely appointed room where his father lay dying.

Anton Costello stirred in his bed. "I knew you would refuse. I. . .I am glad I made my decision."

"What decision?"

"I gave the business to Grant."

Quin stood beside the bed, stone-faced.

"I signed over to him the house, the lands, everything. You will have nothing."

He shook his head and looked away. "Pop, I can't believe you're telling me this. Don't you know that Grant is a slimy. . ."

"He is faithful. You used to be, but something changed in you."

"Yeah, you're right, Pop. Something did change in me. I've seen the light. Hasn't it ever occurred to you that all this activity you've been involved in is wrong? That to persuade these gangs in the inner cities to steal and kill for you is wrong?"

Anton Costello only coughed and turned his head away. After several painful minutes, he said, "I knew you would refuse me. Deep down I knew. I could see that you were not the same devoted son I once loved. You became like Archie, a w-weakling with no sense of getting ahead in the world. I was hoping you would change, but I knew you wouldn't. So I took the necessary steps to prepare." He closed his eyes and appeared to drift off into a restless sleep.

Quin gently shook his father's shoulder. "What? What did you do? Pop, tell me."

"I have already placed Grant in charge of my operations. Even now he has begun the work, starting in Boston. I sent him a few hours ago."

"You sent him to Boston to do what?" Quin again shook his father's shoulder.

"He. . .he will see the Vultures and tell them of the changes." Again his father appeared to have passed out, only to flick his eyes open for a moment. "I trusted you once, but I can't anymore. Another love rules your heart." After this, his father lapsed into a deep sleep.

Quin stared for a moment before leaving the room. At the

far end of the hallway, he caught sight of the trusted butler, Charles, who had been with the family since he was little. Quin stopped the older man and asked him about Grant.

"Yes, Master Costello, Grant is on his way to Boston as we speak. Your father was extremely angry when he heard you had not gone to Paris on your honeymoon. When Grant returned from France, Mr. Costello signed over the business holdings to him in the event of his death. Then just yesterday he was stricken with this illness."

"So Pop knew all along what my answer would be, even when he begged me to reconsider." Quin shook his head, glancing back at the closed doors of the master bedroom. "Even when he's dying he tries to manipulate me, only I find out he has already gone behind my back and arranged everything with that buzzard." After thanking the butler for sharing this information, Quin headed down the stairs and out to the patio. He fell into a wicker chair, suddenly overcome with exhaustion. Everything in his life appeared to be rapidly fading into oblivion. He knew he still had Gail for the time being, but if she were to leave him, he would have nothing left but bitter memories of a corrupt life and a love he could never have.

After a time he heard footsteps approach, and the butler gave him a mournful look.

"Pop's dead?"

"I'm very sorry. If there's anything I can do. . ."

Quin sighed and closed his eyes. For a fleeting moment he felt grief well up within him, only to be replaced by anger at the final words shared between them. He asked if his father had left arrangements for the funeral.

"He wished to be cremated, Master Costello, and his ashes buried next to your mother without a formal ceremony."

A knot formed in Quin's throat as he choked out a feeble,

"Thank you." Now more than ever, he wanted to talk to Gail and feel the comfort of her arms around him. When he called to tell Gail what happened, her sympathy warmed his heart. She asked about the funeral arrangements. Quin responded in a choking voice that his father wished to be cremated without a funeral.

"Oh, Quin, I'm so sorry! Please come here to Boston and be with us. I've been talking to Dorrie. She and Mick really want to meet you."

"I don't know if I can take any religious bombshells right now," he mumbled. "I hurt enough inside as it is."

"They won't do anything like that. They'll just pour out their love. I think it would be good for you. Who knows, maybe you can even go with Mick when he works the streets. He could use a helping hand at the soup kitchen."

Quin suddenly jumped at the sound of the words. "The soup kitchen? You mean his work with the gangs?"

"Yes. In fact Dorrie was just telling me how he's developing relationships with several gang members, particularly with one of the tougher gangs. It's just amazing to see the love Mick has for them after all that's happened."

Quin paced back and forth as his thoughts began to spin. "This gang he's gotten tight with—do you know the name?"

"I think Dorrie called them the Vultures."

His face paled as he withdrew the receiver from his ear. *The Vultures. . .the very gang involved with the business, and Grant is there at this moment!* "Gail, I'm sorry but I've got to go."

"Go where? Quin, what is it? What's the matter?"

Quin threw the phone on the cradle and hastened for his car parked on the circular drive. He heard footsteps pattering on the pavement behind him and whirled to find Andre.

"Sorry, pal, but I have to go," Quin told the hulking figure, still clad in his leather jacket.

"I go, too. We're partners."

Quin shook his head. "Sorry to disappoint you, Andre, but you were right. Grant is in charge of the business now."

Andre's face fell. "You mean he is the boss?"

"Yep, he's the boss all right. Pop turned everything over to him. So I guess you'd better hang out here and wait for Grant to return. Like you told me in Canada, I'm out and he's in."

Andre stared at Quin.

"Look, I gotta run. You take care and don't take any wooden nickels, especially any that Grant gives you. I wouldn't trust him, no way."

Andre pulled out the cash that Quin had given to him on the plane. "No need for the money now. Maybe you need it for your wife?"

Quin stared at the bundle of money in surprise. "Wow, I never thought you had it in you to give back my money. What are you doing in this sad business anyway? It's only for the scum of the earth. Get out while you still can. I should be on my knees, thanking God that He got me out of it. But right now I've got big problems to deal with." He jumped into the car and started the engine, oblivious to the man's somber reaction until the passenger door opened and Andre peered inside.

"What problems?"

"Andre, I have to get going. I have urgent business in Boston."

"Boston? Can I help?"

Quin shook his head. "No, but thanks anyway. I never thought I'd be thanking a big bully in leather. Now I mean it, get out of here while you still can. Things may blow up, and I don't want to see you caught in the middle of it. Do it for your father's memory, if for nothing else."

Andre blinked. "You speak all about fathers. My father was a good man." He then added softly, "He would be angry at what I do. He maybe look down from heaven and say that I am a bad son."

"So you wanna do something good for your pop?"

Andre nodded.

"Maybe I can use you after all. If you really want to help me, get in. I suppose two are better than one in this game." Once Andre was seated, Quin hit the accelerator and sped off.

"I thought you were out of the game?" Andre asked.

"I am. But Grant is deep into it, and there are family members close to my wife who could get hurt. If there's one thing you can do for your pop's memory, Andre, you can help me keep others from getting hurt."

Andre nodded his head. His dark lips curved into a smile. "Yes, this a good thing. I will help others."

twelve

"I can't believe you already have three new members for your Bible study!" Dorrie said happily as she and Gail served chicken salad and croissants for a light supper before Mick left for the evening.

Mick nodded. "Isn't it amazing? Just a week ago, I was moaning to the Lord about my work, and now He suddenly opens heaven's gates. I owe a lot to Corky. He was able to convince some of the Vultures to come, and begged me to hold another study this evening after last night's success."

"Two gatherings in a row!" Dorrie marveled. "It looks like this might turn out to be a fruitful summer for you after all, Mick."

"It sure does," Gail added. When she arrived in Boston, she had been overwhelmed by the love and acceptance poured out by both Dorrie and Mick. She spent long hours conversing with them about everything that had happened since she was married, after which they prayed for Quin and his circumstances.

Mick broke a croissant in two and began eating. "You know, those guys are really hungry for the Word. I have to feed them while their mouths are open—like a big mother bird, I guess you could say."

"I hope you can feed Quin when he comes," Gail said wistfully. "He needs a man to speak to about his life, especially now that his father is gone. He has no family left." She watched Dorrie produce Jamie's dinner from the microwave. The little boy sat in his highchair, pitching cereal onto the linoleum. Gail bent over and picked up the pieces to toss into the garbage. Jamie gurgled and tossed another piece of cereal onto the floor, watching with wide eyes as Gail again picked up the cereal and threw it into the trash. "You aren't going to have anything left to eat if you keep this game up," she remarked to her little nephew. When Dorrie came over with the baby's dinner, Gail whisked the dish from her hands. "Let me try feeding him."

"You sure? I mean, this is baby care, Gail. Are you ready for it?"

"I want to. I have to learn sometime, don't I?" She watched a warm glow of approval cross her sister's face. Picking up the spoon, Gail attempted to place it in Jamie's mouth. The food dribbled down his chin and onto the bib. "Oops."

"It takes some getting used to," Dorrie said. "Keep trying and you'll get the hang of it."

Biting her lip in concentration, Gail spooned up some more food and succeeded in placing it inside Jamie's tiny mouth. "Hurrah! It went in."

"She's already a pro," Mick observed, rising from his seat to stuff his Bible into a day pack. "Well, sorry to eat and run, but I'm already late." He dropped a kiss on Dorrie's cheek before swinging the pack over one shoulder. "Don't wait up for me."

"Have a great time," Dorrie said.

After spooning in the last mouthful of food, Gail wiped off Jamie's mouth with the end of the terry cloth bib and sighed. "There, what do you think of that, Mom?"

"Very good," Dorrie said approvingly. "You have passed a major test in the area of baby nutritional skills."

Jamie giggled in glee before his face scrunched up. After a few minutes, the room filled with the odor of a dirty diaper.

"Well, Gail, are you ready for the next step?" Dorrie inquired with a chuckle.

"You mean changing him? Oh, no, I couldn't."

"Sure you can. Nothing to it." Dorrie plucked Jamie out of the highchair. "Let's head upstairs for the next session of motherhood."

"I don't know about this," Gail answered dubiously, following her sister up the stairs. "I've seen those movies where inexperienced people have tried to put on diapers, only to have the things fall off and the baby doo-doo go all over the place."

Dorrie laughed. "Well, I will teach you how to do it so that won't happen." She went right to work with the baby wipes. "See? You clean him like this," she instructed. "Now here's the diaper. Be sure you put the part of the diaper with the sticky tabs in the back so they wrap around like this."

Gail had fastened one sticky tab when the doorbell rang.

"I'd better go answer the door," Dorrie said as she quickly finished fastening Jamie's diaper before handing him to Gail.

Gail nestled the small boy close to her. In return, he rewarded her with sticky drool on her cheek. "You're such a cute kid," Gail gushed as she slowly walked down the stairs. "Maybe one day I'll have one just like you." She stopped short and gasped at the two men standing in the small foyer of the townhouse. "Quin!"

"When did we get the baby?" he joked, grinning.

Dorrie quickly took the baby before Gail ran to hug Quin. "I missed you so much. How did you know where to find this place?"

"Well," he began, stealing a glance at Dorrie, "I talked to your sister while you were occupied." He stepped back. "I'd like you to meet our bodyguard. This is Andre."

Gail gazed at the huge figure—dressed in a leather jacket— who stood beside Quin. "Our bodyguard?"

"Well, it's a long story."

"I'm so glad I finally get to meet you, Quin!" Dorrie said in glee as she showed the way to the living room. "Unfortunately, my husband, Mick, isn't here right now."

"He's out working the streets," Gail added.

Quin sucked in a breath, glancing at Andre before returning his attention back to the two sisters. "Do you know where he went?"

"Sure. He usually goes to the soup kitchen," Dorrie said, supplementing the information with directions to the establishment. "He told me he's going to have a Bible study with some of the gang members tonight."

"Which gang members are these?"

"The Vultures."

"Then we don't have any time to lose." Quin rose to his feet, motioning to Andre. "Let's go."

"Where are you going, Quin?" Gail asked, her face showing a mixture of confusion and concern.

"Uh, I really want to meet Mick," Quin said, trying to maintain his composure despite his racing heart. "I've heard so much about him, I feel like I know him already. I'm kind of interested in seeing what he does."

"But you just got here."

"Oh, let him go if he wants," Dorrie said, her eyes sparkling at Quin's interest. "I think it's great that Quin wants to check out what Mick's doing with the gangs. And Mick will think God has really opened up some doors."

"Yeah. . .well, we'd better get going." Quin sidestepped his way to the door. "Nice meeting you, Dorrie."

"We'll see you later," she said with a wave.

Once outside, Quin ran to the car, followed by Andre.

"You tell them nothing," Andre observed.

"You're right, I didn't. I wasn't about to tell Dorrie that her husband may be in danger. That's all I need, two sisters in a state of panic. No, it's better that they think Mick's gonna convert me or something."

A few minutes later, Quin and Andre arrived at the soup

kitchen in Boston's inner city. They saw a huge man with ebony-colored skin and wearing a stained apron, working in the kitchen. The man whistled a hymn as he wiped down the stoves and countertops with a sponge. Upon their entrance, he peered through a large open window between the kitchen and the serving area.

"Hey, the kitchen ain't open now."

"We're looking for Mick," Quin said. "Who are you?"

"I'm Harry. Are you dudes here for the Bible study?"

"We really need to find Mick."

"He's at the Vultures' headquarters," the man said matter-of-factly. "Two of them Vultures came here about twenty minutes ago, saying that Mick's friend Corky was out on his feet at the headquarters. Guess he also wants to recruit some more of the brothers to come to our Bible study. You can come too, you know."

"Do you know where the Vultures' headquarters is located?" asked Quin. "I haven't been there in a long time."

The man eyed him curiously. "So you know them Vultures, eh? Man, they're somethin' else, especially the leader of 'em—Odysseus. Man, one time he came in here and showed Mick his switchblade. If that wasn't a scene! Good thing the big man kept his head about it. That's what I like about Mick. He keeps his head in bad situations, and you gotta be able to do that, runnin' a soup kitchen in this 'hood."

Good, Quin thought. *He'll need his head and more if he finds himself tangling with Grant.*

"Anyway," the man continued, "you go down about five blocks, turn left. Look for two black wings spray-painted on the door. Can't miss it."

"Okay, thanks."

Quin and Andre hustled down the dark street. Young people loitered everywhere, on street corners and in dark alleyways. Memories of the times Quin and his father had come here to conduct business haunted Quin. He recalled the eager faces and wide eyes as his father handed the gang members envelopes full of money for the shipments of goods they had confiscated. He knew the young men would run to the nearest drug dealers to spend the money on crack or other illegal drugs. Seeing the empty faces all around him now, Quin could not help but feel a stab of guilt. He and his father had used these kids mercilessly. They had fed the young people's insatiable appetite for drugs and liquor by offering them a deal too good to pass up. As he walked by them, he felt responsible for what they had become—shells of humanity with nothing to live for but the next high or fix.

They arrived at the door with a pair of black wings spray-painted on the rotting wood—the Vultures' lair. Quin motioned to Andre. They scooted down a narrow alleyway running between the buildings until they came to the rear of the structure. At their feet was a milky window, looking in on a room inside the basement. Quin bent down and stared through the dirty glass. A single light bulb, swaying from a frayed cord, illuminated the room. Members of the gang were gathered in small groups; each one wore the customary black leather vest with a vulture embroidered on the back. Most of them were smoking cigarettes or sipping beer from cans.

All at once, the Vultures came to attention when a large man entered the main room. He was wearing a red scarf around his bald head and a sleeveless Vultures jacket that displayed his brawny muscular frame. His fist held a youth by the shirt front. In the rear of the room, like a dark statue, stood a man with raven black hair and a scarred face. A smoking cigarette rested between his fingers. *Grant!*

"You lookin' fer yer brother Corky, Reverend?" the huge man sneered.

Quin stared over at the man they called Reverend. He had a head of blond hair and clutched a book in his hands. *That*

*must be Mick, Gail's brother-in-law. And he's got himself
caught right in the middle of everything. . .just like his father.*

"Please let Corky go, Odysseus," Mick pleaded.

Corky trembled in the leader's grip. "I. . .I didn't say
nuthin'," his voice quivered.

"Shut up!" the man named Odysseus snarled. "It's bad
enough you go leavin' the gang, only to rat on us to the reverend here! Man, you got the guts of a jellyfish, you know
that?"

"I ain't got the guts of no jellyfish!" Corky responded,
only to have the leader shake him.

"Stop it!" Mick cried. "Look, Odysseus, we're only trying
to help you and your brothers."

"Help me, huh?" He eyed the group of men in the room
and began to laugh. All at once the entire room erupted into
raucous laughter. "The reverend here wants to help me? You
should have stayed in your church. Guess you ain't never
learned the lesson from your old man, huh? You see, we
know your old man. He tried to help us, too, and look how
he ended up."

"My father cared for your well-being, like I do," Mick said
in a quiet voice. He held out the book he carried. "You don't
need to keep living like this. Jesus can change your lives. It
says so right here in the Bible."

"I don't want to hear no fool talk about Jesus, Reverend!
You're just like your old man. You don't know when to quit.
You gotta stick your nose where it ain't wanted. That's a real
pity."

"Look, I've got the truth in my hand. Read it for yourself.
The truth in here can set you free from drugs, from the pain
in your past. . . ."

Odysseus marched up and stuck his face into Mick's.
"And I'm tellin' you, I don't want to hear no jive truth from
you or anyone else." Odysseus clamped a firm hand on

Mick's shoulder and spun him around to face the rest of the gang. "You see here? We got ourselves one big problem, brothers. That's this reverend. Man, we gotta do something about this Bible thumpin'." He ripped the Bible from Mick's grasp and began tossing it up in the air like a ball.

"Open it and read what it says, Odysseus," Mick said. "Read and find out for yourself how God loved you enough to—"

The gang leader took the Bible and rammed it into Mick's stomach, sending him reeling to the cement floor. Next, two pairs of hands gripped his arms and thrust him into a wooden chair.

Quin glanced helplessly at Andre. "We've got to do something," he whispered.

"Look, boss, there's Grant," Andre said, pointing. The two men watched as Grant ventured forward, flicking ash from his cigarette onto the cement floor. All the gang members gave him a wide berth as he walked up and surveyed Mick with dark, malevolent eyes.

Grant elbowed Mick. "So, this is the son of that preacher who was shot six years ago?"

"Yeah, that's him all right," Odysseus said. "The high and mighty reverend who quotes the Bible, jus' like his old man. Two peas in a pod."

Grant paced back and forth before Mick. "I hear you know all about the business of the Vultures, thanks to that foolish kid. Eh?" Grant whirled, fixing his gaze on Corky.

"I. . .I'm sorry," Corky said.

"Sorry doesn't repair the damage, though, does it?" Grant drew a pistol from beneath his jacket. He circled behind the chair, jamming the muzzle of the weapon into Mick's head. "Just like your daddy," he murmured. "Sticking your nose in other people's business."

Quin jumped to his feet when he saw what was about to happen. Andre did the same, and slammed his boot through the basement window, shattering it to pieces. The noise sent everyone in the basement whirling around in fear.

"Drop the gun, Grant," Quin ordered as he slid down to the floor, followed by Andre.

Grant lowered the weapon. "Well, well, what a dramatic entrance, young Costello. Back from your honeymoon so soon?" He then eyed Andre, who followed Quin to the floor. "And I see that Andre has brought you. You realize, of course, that you're interfering with important business here."

"You're right, I am." Quin turned to face Odysseus and the Vultures gang. "Look, I'm the son of the big boss-man. Some of you brothers will remember me from when my father came to conduct business here in this 'hood."

"You mean your old man is the big boss we hack all them goods for?" Odysseus asked incredulously. "The one who gave us the cash?"

"That's right."

"You're not in charge anymore, Costello," Grant snarled. "You forfeited your inheritance. Anton Costello placed me in charge. The entire Costello empire is now mine."

"I'm afraid you're mistaken. I'm still the boss's son, right? The legitimate heir to the throne?" He eyed the members of the gang who nodded in agreement.

"Yeah, we know him. He's the boss-man's son, all right," several of the members murmured. "We've seen him around plenty."

"And I told you that *I'm* in charge!" Grant repeated, his voice rising above the murmuring of the Vultures. He rammed his pistol into Mick's skull. Mick winced, then became rigid in the chair as Grant cocked the trigger.

"Now, Costello, you will kindly inform the Vultures here that I am in charge of the business as your father directed, or your wife's brother-in-law dies."

Quin only glared at him. "Yeah, you're in charge all right.

And while we're at it, why don't you tell the Vultures who was in charge six years ago when their former leader took the rap for shooting Mick's father. Tell them who really fired the pistol that day."

"I give the explanations, Costello, not you. Don't you realize that everything you worked for your whole life, everything you ever loved, all belongs to me?"

"Hey now, hold on here," Odysseus interrupted as he came forward. "Just what are you sayin' here, man? You mean Ace didn't shoot that preacher years ago?"

"No," Quin said. "Tell these guys the truth, Grant. Tell them it was you who pulled the trigger, but their brother Ace rots in jail to pay for your crime."

"I don't need to, Costello, because your time is up." Grant aimed his weapon at Quin. Andre lunged for Grant, firmly grasping the wrist that held the gun. The two men struggled. As they did, a shot rang out. Grant fell to the ground, gasping as a crimson stain spread across his shirt. A wisp of smoke curled out of the weapon Andre held in his hand. Shock enveloped the man's face as he hurled the weapon to the ground and bolted for the door.

Quin stood over his dying enemy, watching the man heave for air. As he did, he heard a choked whisper. "Y–you think you have won the. . .the game. You. . .you don't know who it was who destroyed the Costellos, one by one." Grant squeezed his eyes shut, then flicked them open to stare at the ceiling above.

Quin's eyes widened. "What are you saying, Grant? That you're responsible?"

"All of them," Grant whispered. "Archie, Treva. . .the big man h–himself. . . . The proud Costellos. . .gone." He smiled faintly. "All but you. I almost had you, too. But I have my reward." With his last breath he sputtered, "You will live with this for the rest of your life."

"No!" Quin collapsed next to his enemy, shaking the dead form. "No!"

Suddenly the headquarters were swarming with uniformed police officers and detectives, their sidearms drawn. The Vultures who did not escape the authorities were quickly handcuffed. A detective drew Quin up by his arm, hurling questions into his face. Quin never heard the voice barking at him as he stood frozen in place, staring at the face of his enemy while his confession reverberated in Quin's mind. *Grant killed my family. Grant is responsible for everything*.

The officer searched Quin's pockets, and finding a license bearing his name, pushed Quin to the wall. "Spread them right now, pal. Hands behind your head."

Hands frisked him quickly before his wrists were forced into a pair of steel handcuffs. Another officer rattled off his rights.

At that moment Mick came forward. "You don't need to arrest him, officer," Mick stated. "He and this man here. . . ," he pointed to Andre, who had already been handcuffed outside the building, "they saved my life."

"Even if they did do one good thing," the officer responded, "it doesn't erase years of criminal activity. We've been looking to bust up this syndicate for a long time. And this one," the detective ruffled Quin's shirt, "is a ring leader in the operation. He's wanted in at least five other states. Aren't you, pal?"

Quin said nothing. Mick stared at Quin, who looked straight back without flinching. Mick opened his mouth as if about to say something, but never had the opportunity as the police pushed Quin out the door.

thirteen

"I still can't believe this happened," Dorrie said softly as she sat with Gail and Mick around the kitchen table late that night. "I mean, this type of thing only happens in the movies."

Gail had sat in silence since hearing the news of Quin's arrest. While it pained her to know that Quin and his father were involved in a huge crime syndicate that used gangs in the inner cities to make money, her heart nevertheless was drawn to the man now sitting in some lonely cell. She listened, numb, as Mick and Dorrie rehashed the events of the evening; she absently twisted the wedding rings around and around on her left hand.

"I tell you, I owe both those men my life," Mick said, his blue eyes acknowledging the somber Gail. "Of course, at the time of the incident, I had no idea he was your husband."

"He's not. . .not really," Gail said quietly.

"What do you mean he's not?" asked Dorrie. "Of course he is."

"Dorrie, I don't even know who he is. I thought I did, but he hid himself behind this mask of Keith Hampton, a man I thought I loved. I told him in Canada that I married Keith Hampton, not Quintin Costello." She sniffed as tears rolled down her cheeks. "Now I find out he's a criminal, involved in some syndicate run by his father! Oh, how I wish I could have my sweet Keith back again. I'd do anything! *He* is the man I love with all my heart."

Dorrie placed an arm around Gail, who had begun to cry for the umpteenth time since discovering what had been

150

concealed from her until this night. Despite the pain, she realized why Quin hid the circumstances surrounding his family. He had warned her countless times of the danger, but she never fully understood what he had meant until now.

A strong hand suddenly gripped Gail's hand. She looked up to see Mick staring at her. "Gail, I know you've been hurt by Quin. But I believe God is trying to change his heart. Don't you see? If he was so wrapped up in his father's lucrative business, why would he risk everything to save someone like me? I was a threat to all of them after Corky told me about their shady business. That man called Grant would have killed me, and possibly Corky, too, if Quin and the other man had not shown up when they did."

Gail sniffed as Dorrie pressed a tissue into her hand. She smiled her thanks before blowing her nose.

"Yeah, he's blown it big time," Mick continued, "but so have the rest of us in one way or another. You remember how I turned my back on God after what happened to my father? In God's eyes, what Quin has done is no worse than what I did. But what's truly amazing is that God can redeem us through what His Son did on the cross. I think it would be wrong for you or me to write Quin off just because he's in jail."

Gail dabbed her eyes with the tissue. "Do you think I should try calling him?"

"I'm going to find out if he has a lawyer and see if there's a way we can communicate with him as soon as possible. I owe Quin my life, but more importantly, I want him to know that someone also gave His life for him. I want to see him made whole; I want him to receive the gift of salvation that we all have."

Gail nodded. "Maybe God can still perform a miracle in his heart, especially after everything that's happened. I know he hurts inside. I've seen his pain. I guess it would be wrong not to be there for him."

"The Bible talks about going to see those who are in prison," Dorrie agreed. "We should be willing to do all we can to see this man set free, not only from jail, but from sin as well."

❧

Quin sat in the small holding cell, waiting for something to happen. The family lawyer, George Rawlings, had been by to see him earlier that morning, but did not offer him much hope. "We'll first have to see what happens at your arraignment later today, and then the preliminary hearing," the lawyer had said matter-of-factly as he stuffed a file folder into his leather briefcase. "With your father dead, it's likely the district attorney will seek to place the blame on you, painting you as a dangerous criminal requiring incarceration."

"If I'm denied bond, that means I'm stuck here?"

"Afraid so. The preliminary hearing will be to determine if there is enough evidence to certify the charges to a grand jury. If the grand jury indicts you, which is likely, then you're looking at a trial in a year, maybe two. The delay will be due to your involvement in other states. It's going to take time to gather all the evidence. I'm hoping to have everything take place here in Boston, rather than have you extradited all over the country."

Quin paced back and forth before the wealthy lawyer dressed in a pinstriped suit. "Okay, so lay it on me straight. What are my chances in all of this?"

"Our first order of business is to get you out on bail. That will free you for the time being. More than likely, the grand jury will indict you on the charges specified, with the evidence already secured by the district attorney."

"But I'm not guilty of half the charges they've leveled on me, especially that second degree murder rap. I've never hurt anyone in my life!"

"That may be, but the district attorney's office is gathering evidence of your involvement in your father's operations. I'll be frank with you, Quintin. It will be a long road if you choose to plead not guilty and proceed with a trial."

"What other choice is there but a trial? I mean, look at the murderers who have gotten off. All I know is I'm not guilty of a lot of those charges. I think a trial is my best chance."

"Well, a trial is never set in stone. After what you've told me about your marriage, and how you intervened on behalf of your wife's brother-in-law during the scuffle with the Vultures gang, I believe it's possible to sway a jury member. But I'm not optimistic. I believe entering into a plea bargain might be a viable option in your case. There are many others involved in this syndicate that the police would love to get their hands on. You have the information they need to make more arrests."

"I don't know what they want," Quin said glumly. "I can hardly remember who I am anymore."

"Well, you'd better come up with the information they want, because if you're convicted, you're looking at a pretty stiff sentence."

"Okay, so say I plead not guilty and go ahead with a trial. What then?"

"If you are found guilty on all counts, the prosecution will try to impose the maximum sentence."

"Which is what?"

Rawlings sighed, his face serious. "It's entirely possible you're looking at a life sentence. Possible parole after thirty years."

❧

Life in prison. Life behind bars. The words echoed over and over in his mind as he rested on the hard bed in the corner of the cell. His hands ran through his hair. *Me, Quintin Costello—a jailbird at twenty-eight.* He thought of Gail then as he felt his left ring finger that no longer wore the wedding band they had purchased together in Poughkeepsie only a few weeks ago. *Gail will never forgive me for all the lies, the deceit, and the pain I caused her.* Again he brushed back strands of his dark hair. *It's probably better for her if I stay locked up. I might as well plead guilty and get the sentencing over with. Gail will not want anything more to do with me. My family's gone. There's no one waiting for me outside these concrete walls.* He slumped his head into his hands when he thought of Grant's dying words about the death of Quin's family members. Anger welled up in him; it was directed toward his deceased father for hiring such a despicable man. *How could you have done this to us, Pop? To me, to our family? How could you have allowed our family to be destroyed by Grant, all for the sake of your empire?*

Quin lifted his head at the sound of a security officer unlocking his cell. "C'mon Costello, you have a phone call."

His eyes widened as he followed the officer through the hallways. *Who could possibly want to talk to me?*

&

Gail sat nervously at the kitchen table, trying to steady her jittery knees. *Why am I doing this?* she thought lamely. The notion of calling a place where criminals were housed felt like something she should be watching on a television drama. Never would she have guessed she would so much as *talk* with a man arrested for serious crimes, let alone be married to such a man. Yet she could not help but call Quin after watching the news footage of police guiding him into the station, his wrists handcuffed behind his back. His face appeared mournful, his shoulders hunched over as if he carried the weight of the world on them. When Gail saw him, she knew she still loved him, no matter what he had done.

Gail grew rigid in her seat when a soft hello came over the

phone. Her heart flipped within her.

"You have five minutes," she heard the guard say.

Gail moaned softly. Five minutes to tell Quin everything that was brewing within her heart. "Hi, Quin. How are you?"

Quin cleared his throat and mumbled, "I don't know."

"Well, I'm calling to tell you I still love you, despite what's happened."

Quin chuckled. "Right. Ol' Jailbird Costello."

"No, I love Quintin Costello. And I'm going to do everything I can to help you."

She heard a soft sigh. "Look, Gail, I'm really sorry about all this. I never should have talked you into marrying me. I was selfish. I knew from the beginning it was a mistake. I wanted to make you mine and I didn't care if you got hurt in the process. So you might as well take the rings off and sell them. It's over between us."

"I can't take them off."

"Yes, you can. I'm a hardened criminal. My lawyer says there's no hope. I could get life behind bars after all is said and done."

The weight of that statement caught her off guard. She wrestled with the idea of him in prison for the rest of his life until the reason for her call overshadowed her apprehension. "I want to tell you what I've been thinking." Gail inhaled a deep breath. "I won't lie to you. This whole situation has really shaken me. I know you dropped hints about your family, but wouldn't tell me the truth. And I realize that if I did know about your family, it might have put me in danger. You were only trying to protect me, like what you and that bodyguard did for Mick."

She was met with silence. She went on. "You have a lot of love in you, Quin, and a heart that wants to do the right things. But I found out that we really don't have the strength to do what's right. We need God to help us. Inside all of us are bad thoughts, selfishness, pride. All of us should be in jail cells right now."

"Yeah, but you're not," he said pointedly. "You're free."

"You can't really be free unless you have Jesus inside you. In this world you will always do wrong. But I found out something while we were on our honeymoon. I found out that with God in my heart, my old self really did pass away and a new self has been born. When I stared at those mountains, I felt like I was actually seeing them for the first time. It really felt like I had been born all over again. We talked about that, remember?"

"Yeah, I remember."

"Well, that's what it means to be a Christian, Quin. You're born again into the kingdom of God where He forgives all your past mistakes. You really feel new on the inside."

"So is that why you called, to clean me up?"

"No. I called to say I love you and I want to know what is happening. Do you have a trial or something coming up?"

"My arraignment is this afternoon."

"What does that mean?"

"Well, if the judge agrees to set bond and I post it, then I'm out of here until the preliminary hearing."

"And if he doesn't?"

"Then I'll rot in jail for the rest of my life and you'll never have to deal with me again."

The phone clicked in her ear, the line dead. Gail sat still, numbed by his callous response. She replaced the receiver and stood. Bright sunshine filtered through the kitchen window on a crystal clear day. "No, you're not going to rot in jail, Quintin Costello. Even though you don't believe me, I do still love you and somehow, with God's help, we're going to pray you out of that place."

❧

Mick, Dorrie, and Gail arrived at the courthouse where the arraignment had already concluded. Reporters swarmed about them like a flock of sea gulls after a bucket of fish; they were looking for anything they could splash across the tabloids and TV screen. Mick provided a quick statement to the press before ushering the sisters into the building. As Gail climbed the last set of steps, she heard a woman reporter ask her why she decided to marry a corrupt man who was part of a crime operation that had stayed ahead of the authorities for years. Gail's face burned with embarrassment as Dorrie shielded her with an arm.

"Dorrie, how can I get through this?" Gail whispered in fear. She clung to Dorrie's hand, heaving quick breaths while trying to maintain her composure. She knew the time of reckoning had passed. Either she would have Quin in her arms very soon, or she would only glimpse his sad face as he sat in a dreary prison.

"It's going to be okay," Dorrie assured her. "God is with us. He will never forsake us."

In the hallway before the wide oak doors leading into the courtroom, Gail noticed a lawyer conversing with court officials. The man glanced up, then nodded his head to the officials before striding over to shake Mick's hand. "I recognize your face from the newspaper. We've talked on the phone," he said, introducing himself as Quin's lawyer, George Rawlings.

"Thank you, sir. This is my wife, Dorrie, and Quin's wife, Gail."

"Glad to see you all here. I know Quintin values your support. The going won't be easy for him. I am happy to report, however, that we were successful in getting the judge to set bail."

Gail turned and gave Dorrie a hug. Mick was all smiles as

he wrapped his arms around the celebrating sisters. "God can perform miracles," Mick told the lawyer. "While we believe in justice, we also believe that Quin's heart has changed. His activities during the last year prove that he knew his father's business dealings were wrong. He risked his life to try and stop it. We prayed for leniency. Thank you, Lord."

"So what happened, Mr. Rawlings?" Gail asked.

"Well, the charges were brought before the judge. The district attorney tried his best to deny Quintin bond, citing the family's history of extensive travel and their criminal activity. It was heavy going there for a while. The judge heard about what happened last evening with the gang, and Quintin's involvement, and I believe that swayed him to set the bond at two hundred and fifty thousand dollars."

"Wow, that's a lot of money," Mick whistled. "Can Quin can up with it?"

"He has a trust fund worth over a million that I will access immediately. But this is the first of many steps in a long legal battle, I'm afraid. I wish I could convince him to enter into a plea bargain agreement that might prove better for him than standing trial. I'm sure I can count on all of you to help Quintin. I will need your sworn testimonies in future proceedings."

"You can count on us, sir," Mick assured him. "All of us will help in any way we can. We'll take it one step at a time. Thank you for your efforts, Mr. Rawlings."

"Well, I must say, this young man is fortunate to have you three. I was saddened to hear about the tragedy concerning his family. It's good to know that he has friends waiting for him when he gets out. I'll be in touch." Rawlings shook their hands before glancing at his watch. "I'd better get over to the bank and arrange for the bail money. We'll have Quintin out by the end of the day."

Gail hugged both Dorrie and Mick, thankful for this small victory in the shadow of greater battles yet to be fought.

fourteen

"Why do you want to go through with this?" Quin asked Gail after she returned from running her errands to various shops scattered around the small Massachusetts town.

She smiled as she displayed her purchases of garland, crepe wedding bells, plates, cups, and napkins. "It won't be much," she confessed, "but I'm thankful that everything seems to be falling into place."

Quin shook his head and thrust his hands into his pockets before strolling over to a window to look at the scenery. He was grateful for the small apartment Mick and Dorrie had secured for them in a small New England town outside of Boston, away from all the publicity surrounding his arrest. Quin could not help but marvel at Gail's love and devotion to him since his release. Internally, he felt burdened by the guilt of his past, but Gail proceeded on with life's activities as if nothing adverse had happened.

"So do your parents plan on attending?" Quin asked.

"Of course. Dad has to give me away, you know."

"I don't believe it. Why are they allowing their daughter to go through with a church wedding to a dangerous criminal? I mean, you heard what the district attorney said on television— I'm a detriment to society."

Gail reached over and placed a warm hand on his arm. "Quin, my folks know we have said our vows to one another before the justice of the peace. They're glad we want to be married in a church before witnesses and especially before God."

"Yeah, but that doesn't erase who I am or the kind of life I once led."

"No, it doesn't. But you know who *can* erase the wrongs in your past and leave you with peace, Quin."

He continued to stare out the window, watching a robin flutter down to the small patch of grass outside the apartment. The bird hopped along on its clawed feet, searching for worms among the fallen leaves. Soon the robin would fly south to avoid the cold winter that would blanket the ground with freshly fallen snow. As each day passed, Quin wrestled with his own winter, and the raw conviction hanging over him. Mick spent time showing him the Scriptures and dealing with his heart, but somehow Quin felt beyond repair. There was still the preliminary hearing and an eventual trial ahead, even though his lawyer continually badgered him to make a plea bargain. Now, as Gail happily pounced on the plan to have a real wedding ceremony, he held to his reservations.

"Look, Gail, I can't do this to you and your family," he finally said. "You should just forget about me and find someone else who won't become a jailbird in a year or two."

To his surprise, Gail came and laid her curly head against his shoulder. "Quin, there isn't anyone else. There never will be."

"But how can you marry me, knowing I'll likely be serving time behind bars? You can't have a marriage like that."

"I can because I love you and I know that love is greater than any jail cell. I'll be thankful to God for any time I can spend with you. Now I have to go pick up something at Dorrie's. I'll be back in a little bit."

After Gail departed, Quin replayed the conversation in his mind. He wished he had the same peace and confidence that strengthened her. He found that turmoil, doubt, and anger, combined with his faults, had poisoned his soul. Yet, he had witnessed how Gail changed dramatically under the hand of God. She accepted Quin unconditionally, despite his criminal wrongdoing. He picked up the phone to dial Mick's number, wondering if he might find a similar peace in the midst of his difficulties.

Dorrie came into the living area where Gail lay on the floor bouncing a little clown in front of Jamie, who giggled with delight. "I thought you told me you couldn't handle kids," she commented with a chuckle.

Gail glanced up and smiled. "This is a cute kid you've got, Dorrie. I'm a lucky aunt."

"And he's a blessed nephew," Dorrie said, scooping Jamie into her arms and cuddling him close. "I think you'll be even more blessed when I tell you the news."

"What?"

"Mick's been on the phone upstairs for over an hour, talking to—"

"Quin?" Gail leapt to her feet, ready to dash to the kitchen where the extension phone rested in its cradle on the wall. "I have to talk to him!"

"Hey, now wait a minute," Dorrie called to her. "It's better to leave them alone and let God work on Quin's heart."

"Oh, Dorrie, do you think. . . ?"

Her sister winked. "It looks real good. Praise the Lord!"

Just then Mick came bounding down the stairs, his face beaming as he gave each sister a hug. "I am pleased to announce that the Holy Spirit has just birthed a bouncing new baby Christian."

"Oh, Mick!" Gail cried. "Quin gave his life to the Lord?"

"Every bit of it. Other than myself, I never heard a man cry like he did. He laid everything on the altar tonight—his family, his past, and the whole trial next year. I know something special happened in his heart."

"I have to go see him!" Gail announced, racing for the front door.

"Gail, wait a minute," Dorrie hollered before Mick caught her arm and shook his head.

"Let them celebrate, Dorrie. This is their time to rejoice."

She sighed. "You're right. This is a night to celebrate a new life born into the kingdom of God. Right, little Jamie?"

The baby stared at her with his dark brown eyes, then laughed along with his parents.

≥≈

Gail drove up the street, her heart bursting with joy. For weeks she had held Quin up in prayer, and now her prayers had been answered. Autumn leaves swirled in a frenzy as the automobile drove by trees painted bright orange and red. She stopped before the brick apartment building, jumped out of the car, and raced for the door. She paused when she heard footsteps approaching from the sidewalk.

"Looking for someone?" a deep voice inquired.

She whirled to find Quin there with a grin on his face.

Gail threw her arms around him. "Oh, Quin! Mick told me what happened."

"Yeah," he said, nuzzling his face into her curls. "I just had to take a walk around the block. Like you told me at Lake Louise, everything looks so new and different—the trees, the birds, the way the clouds move across the sky. I see everything in a new and different way now. I guess this is what it's like to be born again."

Gail stepped back to see the joy radiating in his face. Impulsively, she leaned over and kissed him. The contact startled him before he responded with enthusiasm. When they parted, Gail asked if he now felt comfortable proceeding with the wedding plans.

"With everything that is in me and more," he told her. He went on to share his conversation with Mick. "The greatest revelation came to me after I shared my thoughts about being a criminal. I told Mick that God wouldn't have anything to do with a criminal. Mick said that wasn't true. Jesus knew criminals well. He was crucified with two of them. One ridiculed him, but the other was promised a place in Paradise.

He said if Jesus could find a place in Paradise for a criminal, he could certainly find a place for me in His kingdom."

"That's great! I knew Mick would say the right things."

"He really does have a gift for reaching the needy," Quin agreed as they walked down a side street arm in arm, watching the leaves dance about in the breeze. "And it looks like you're going to get your fall wedding after all. I just wish. . . ," he paused and closed his eyes.

"What?"

"You know we won't have a lot of time together, Gail. I'll soon be hip deep in all the legal troubles related to the trial, and then. . .well, who knows what will happen. I could be in jail for a long time."

"Have you considered this plea bargaining that the lawyer suggested?"

Quin shrugged as he scuffed up a few leaves lying on the pavement. "I've thought about it. But it means mandatory jail time, no matter what. At least with a jury trial, I have the chance of an acquittal."

"But you know that won't happen."

Quin nodded. "There's plenty of evidence stacked up against me, and some angry people who'll say anything to get me locked up for good."

"Then it looks like a plea bargain may be your only choice, Quin," she said softly.

He turned and gathered her into his arms, holding her as if he never wanted to let go. "Then I will be away from you. If there's any chance I can keep that from happening. . ."

"You'll never be away from my heart. Even if prison bars separate us, it will only be for a time. Meanwhile, we're together right now. So let's make the most of it."

"Okay," he said softly before kissing her lips that tasted sweeter than clover honey.

❧

Gail stood nervously in front of the mirror as Dorrie adjusted the veil on her head and pinned it into place with several bobby pins. "Gail, you keep jumping around, and this thing will be sitting crooked on your little head."

"It's bridal shakes."

"Isn't it funny that there is such a thing as bridal shakes?" Dorrie slid the last pin into place, then stepped back to observe the effect. "Perfect. You look lovely."

Gail examined the long white dress in the mirror, marveling that her mother had decided to hold on to the dress she had originally picked out at the bridal shop. The beadwork glistened in the lights of the room. "I'm so thankful your pastor decided to officiate, Dorrie."

"He was quite touched when Mick explained everything. When he had the chance to meet you and Quin in that private counseling session, he knew that God had placed you two together for a special purpose."

Gail again looked at her reflection in the mirror before ordering her sister to find her a tube of lipstick.

"Just don't get any of it on your dress," Dorrie laughed, handing her a tube.

Gail traced the color along her lips. "There!" she said. "That's something I didn't give up after becoming a Christian. I still like my makeup."

"I think God will overlook that minor quirk in your life," Dorrie joked with a laugh before picking up her bouquet. At that moment Mick entered; he was dressed in his tuxedo, to stand as Quin's best man. In his arms he held little Jamie, decked out in a blue velvet suit and matching blue bow tie.

"Are you ready?" Mick asked.

"She's ready and she looks lovely," Dorrie answered before Gail could open her mouth.

"So do you," Mick told Dorrie, giving her a quick peck on

the lips. "I like seeing you in a fancy dress."

"Well, get yourself a high-paying faculty job at school, then you can buy me loads of party dresses."

"Maybe I will," he said with a grin. "I like the effect it's having on me."

Dorrie shook her head. "No, Mick. God's called you to a higher purpose. He's looking for men willing to throw caution to the wind to reach those in need. I'm so glad you decided to go on with your work at the soup kitchen."

"Yeah," he said softly. "We've had quite a rise in attendance since the whole escapade."

Gail glanced over. "Really?"

"You should see the guys strutting in now, wanting to catch a glimpse of the man who faced the Vultures gang. All the news coverage has increased our contributions to the soup kitchen, both in donated food and money. Believe it or not, the whole thing opened up the ministry like never before."

They walked out to the foyer together. The open doors of the sanctuary revealed an arrangement of carnations sitting in front of the podium, and pews decorated with white satin bows. "Well, Mick, if God has opened the door, then you would be foolish not to enter, right?" Dorrie gestured inside the church. "Look what awaits you. Heaven's glory. The sanctuary of God. 'For a day in Your courts is better than a thousand,' " she concluded, quoting from Psalms.

He gave her a loving squeeze. "That's what I love about you. You have a unique grasp on God and His word that always amazes me. It amazed me even when my heart was far from Him."

"God amazes me how He can take people like us and use us to do His will."

"Amen."

"And I second that," Gail said with a smile. She inhaled a

deep breath to steady her nervous tremors and turned to see her father enter the foyer, dressed in his tuxedo. He stood still and silent, staring at her, until he came forward to bestow a hug.

"Your mother is still trying to pin on her corsage without crying," he chuckled. "But you look perfect."

"That's what Dorrie said," Gail noted. "I told her once that you and her are both alike in many ways."

"Well, I'm very proud of my daughter."

Gail stared into her father's eyes. "Are you, Dad? You're not upset about Quin, especially after all that's happened?"

"Well, it was a struggle for me at first," he admitted. "The idea of my little girl running off with a criminal is not the sort of thing a father wishes for his daughter. But after talking with Dorrie and Mick and seeing the big picture for myself, your young man is willing to try to overcome his mistakes. I'm sad that you two will be apart for so long, but you know the saying—absence makes the heart grow fonder." He hugged her once more. "I'm only glad you finally decided to go through with this ceremony. I'll have to admit, it does make me consider what you two girls have done by giving your lives to God. I see changes in both of you that would have never come about unless something greater than you was at work." He added with chuckle, "It wasn't just your upbringing, either."

"Hey, Dad? Mick is wonderful at helping men understand about God."

Her father winked. "Ah-ha, I knew you would say something like that. Well, we'll talk about it after the ceremony." He offered her his arm. "Right now, I think you have an anxious groom waiting for you."

Gail smiled and tucked her hand in the crook of his elbow, breathing deeply to calm her jitters. Her dream of a wedding had finally come true. Gail and her father walked down the aisle before the well-wishers, gathered together as witnesses. The wedding dress and long train swept the floor while organ music played the processional. Her eyes rose to meet the warm smile on Quin's face as he stood ready to receive her as his wife before the eyes of God.

Afterward there were cheese and fruit trays at the simple reception, along with a wedding cake. Gail relished every minute of the festivities as she clung to Quin's arm while mingling with the guests. She enjoyed the moment when they took up the knife in both their hands and slowly cut a piece of the cake. The simple wedding wasn't the elaborate creation she had once envisioned, but she was thankful for all that God had done in bringing her together with the one man who occupied her thoughts every moment of the day.

~

Quin and Gail rode back to the apartment in his car, which was painted up with the words "Just Married"; the ride was made all the more interesting by the tinkling of tin cans fastened beneath the bumper. Quin jumped out and yanked open the passenger door.

"I wish we were leaving on our honeymoon tomorrow," he announced as they walked up to the apartment door. He shook his head. "Life is sure different now, isn't it?"

Gail looked at him and the sudden sadness overshadowing him. "Quin, what's the matter?"

"I'm just thinking about all the things I could have given you if my family and I had made honest money like normal people. Now all I have to look forward to is a criminal trial and lawyers' fees. There's no money for that trip to Europe like you wanted."

"I'm just thankful to finally have the real you."

"Are you?"

"Quin, we're now real people. We aren't pretending anymore, or living double lives. We can be the people God meant for us to be, and enjoy each other while we have time."

"It was all pretty confusing," he said, stepping up to the apartment door and unlocking it. He looked over at her and extended his arms. "Now that the confusion has passed, we can take the next step."

"What do you mean? What are you doing?"

"We've never had the chance to perform this custom. Come here."

Gail looked at him quizzically until he scooped her up in his arms.

"Quin!" she shouted, batting him playfully on his chest. "Put me down!"

"I'm supposed to carry you over the threshold, Mrs. Costello."

"I just hope no one's looking," she mumbled in embarrassment as he carried her into the apartment.

Once inside, she gasped at the huge bouquet of long-stemmed red roses waiting for her on the table, accompanied by a pair of candlesticks that he lit with a match. "Oh, it's beautiful!"

"Just like you."

Gail stared at the man to whom she had exchanged her heartfelt vows, watching the candlelight illuminate his features and his eyes reflect the flame. His entire face glowed with the eternal light of Christ in his heart, and with a deep abiding love for her. Now as they came together to share in a kiss, Gail was thankful to finally know the real man she had married.

epilogue

The wind swept across his face, blowing his fine brown hair. The sky appeared unnaturally bright, with an expanse of turquoise blue stretching from one horizon to the other. He had not seen so much sky in years. Birds clinging to tree limbs sang songs of welcome. Flowers scented the air. Freedom never felt so good to his weary bones as he slowly walked across the pavement toward a set of benches shaded by a large maple tree.

Suddenly, he heard a sound rise up as the wind. It was soft at first, like a whisper, then grew louder as he walked.

"Daddy! Oh, Daddy!"

He squinted. A young girl raced toward him, her arms outstretched. Her cheeks were rosy red, her smile radiant. Could it be?

"Daddy!" the young girl cried again before her tiny arms looped around his thin form in a fierce hug.

He nuzzled his face into her curly brown hair. "Grace," he whispered. "How I missed you. I. . .I missed everything— your first bite of cereal, your first steps, your first words. Now look at you." He stepped back to survey the pretty young thing with deep brown eyes like her parents. "Why, you're nine years old."

She clasped his hand in hers, swinging it back and forth.

Tears welled up in his eyes and dribbled down his cheeks. "I missed out on so much because of all my mistakes. Oh, Lord, how can You redeem the time I have lost?"

A vision of beauty in the distance caught his attention. It

was a vision like so many he had imagined while living day after day in a concrete cell, thinking of all he was missing in life. Only this time, the vision of a beautiful woman with curly hair that whipped in the wind was real. A smile appeared on the soft oval face as she approached.

"You're real," he said out loud. "You're not just a dream."

"Yes, I'm real." She came forward and kissed him tenderly. "I'm very real. God heard our prayers. He set my captive free."

"Yes." He ran his fingers through the curly hair he could only dream about while in his cell. The hair felt like silk to his touch. "Thank You, God. . .for my family," he managed to say, his voice choking with emotion.

"Grace, you hold Daddy's hand and I'll hold the other one. We have a nice welcome-home dinner planned, just the three of us."

He smiled as his family led him to a waiting car. After ten long years, Quintin Costello walked away from the huge brick buildings and barbed-wire fencing of the correctional facility, grateful for the power of love that had set him free.

A Letter To Our Readers

Dear Reader:

In order that we might better contribute to your reading enjoyment, we would appreciate your taking a few minutes to respond to the following questions. We welcome your comments and read each form and letter we receive. When completed, please return to the following:

Rebecca Germany, Fiction Editor
Heartsong Presents
PO Box 719
Uhrichsville, Ohio 44683

1. Did you enjoy reading *Behind the Mask?*
    ❏ Very much. I would like to see more books
    by this author!
    ❏ Moderately
    I would have enjoyed it more if _____

    _____

    _____

2. Are you a member of **Heartsong Presents**? Yes ❏ No ❏
    If no, where did you purchase this book? _____

    _____

3. How would you rate, on a scale from 1 (poor) to 5 (superior),
    the cover design? _____

4. On a scale from 1 (poor) to 10 (superior), please rate the
    following elements.

    _____ Heroine   _____ Plot

    _____ Hero   _____ Inspirational theme

    _____ Setting   _____ Secondary characters

5. These characters were special because_____

_____

_____

6. How has this book inspired your life?_____

_____

_____

7. What settings would you like to see covered in future
   Heartsong Presents books?_____

_____

_____

8. What are some inspirational themes you would like to see
   treated in future books?_____

_____

_____

9. Would you be interested in reading other **Heartsong
   Presents** titles?   Yes ❑   No ❑

10. Please check your age range:
    ❑ Under 18   ❑ 18-24   ❑ 25-34
    ❑ 35-45   ❑ 46-55   ❑ Over 55

11. How many hours per week do you read?_____

Name _____

Occupation _____

Address _____

City _____ State _____ Zip _____

Classic Romance

From the grande dame of Christian romance, Grace Livingston Hill, comes this exciting collection—featuring three stories from Grace Livingston Hill and a bonus novel from Isabella Alden, Grace Livingston Hill's aunt and a beloved writer herself.

Collection #2 includes the complete Grace Livingston Hill books *Lone Point*, *Because of Stephen*, and *The Story of a Whim*.

450 pages, Paperback, 5 ³/₁₆" x 8"

❦ ❦ ❦ ❦ ❦ ❦ ❦ ❤ ❦ ❦ ❦ ❦ ❦ ❦ ❦

❦ ❦ ❦ ❦ ❦ ❦ ❦ ❤ ❦ ❦ ❦ ❦ ❦ ❦ ❦

Heartsong

······Presents······

Great Inspirational Romance at a Great Price!

Heartsong Presents books are inspirational romances in contemporary and historical settings, designed to give you an enjoyable, spirit-lifting reading experience. You can choose wonderfully written titles from some of today's best authors like Veda Boyd Jones, Yvonne Lehman, Tracie Peterson, Debra White Smith, and many others.

When ordering quantities less than twelve, above titles are $2.95 each.
Not all titles may be available at time of order.

Hearts♥ng Presents

Love Stories Are Rated G!

That's for godly, gratifying, and of course, great! If you love a thrilling love story, but don't appreciate the sordidness of some popular paperback romances, **Heartsong Presents** is for you. In fact, **Heartsong Presents** is the *only inspirational romance book club*, the only one featuring love stories where Christian faith is the primary ingredient in a marriage relationship.

Sign up today to receive your first set of four, never before published Christian romances. Send no money now; you will receive a bill with the first shipment. You may cancel at any time without obligation, and if you aren't completely satisfied with any selection, you may return the books for an immediate refund!

Imagine. . .four new romances every four weeks—two historical, two contemporary—with men and women like you who long to meet the one God has chosen as the love of their lives. . .all for the low price of $9.97 postpaid.

To join, simply complete the coupon below and mail to the address provided. **Heartsong Presents** romances are rated G for another reason: They'll arrive *Godspeed!*